THE REFERENCE SHELF

REPRESENTATIVE
AMERICAN SPEECHES
1980–1981

Edited by Owen Peterson
Professor, Department of Speech
Louisiana State University

THE REFERENCE SHELF

Volume 53, Number 5

THE H. W. WILSON COMPANY

New York   1981

THE REFERENCE SHELF

The books in this series contain reprints of articles, excerpts from books, and addresses on current issues and social trends in the United States and other countries. There are six separately bound numbers in each volume, all of which are generally published in the same calendar year. One number is a collection of recent speeches; each of the others is devoted to a single subject and gives background information and discussion from various points of view, concluding with a comprehensive bibliography. Books in the series may be purchased individually or on subscription.

Library of Congress Cataloging in Publication Data

Main entry under title:

Representative American speeches, 1980–1981.

(The Reference shelf ; v. 53, no. 5)
Includes index.
1. United States—Politics and government—1977–1981—Sources. 2. American oratory—20th century. I. Peterson, Owen, 1924–   . II. Series.
E872.R46   973.926   81–16070
ISBN 0–8242–0657–6   AACR2

International Standard Book Number 0–8242–0657–6
PRINTED IN THE UNITED STATES OF AMERICA

CONTENTS

3

4 The Reference Shelf

PREFACE

American public address in 1980–1981 reflected the three main areas of concern in the country that dominated headlines and evening news telecasts: the election, the economy, and the American hostages in Iran.

The government's inability to reverse the downward economic spiral and find a solution to the energy crisis, not new problems, were coupled with frustration over its failure to secure release of the hostages in Iran and exacerbated a national feeling of futility. Well-intentioned gimmicks designed to rally public support for the hostage release, such as the display of flags and yellow ribbons and nightly television news reminders of the number of days in captivity, served to remind Americans of their country's helplessness. The feeling inevitably spilled over into the election, influencing its outcome.

On the whole, the election campaign rhetoric was neither inspiring nor memorable. The sheer length of the campaign militated against eloquence. When Philip Crane made the first official announcement of his candidacy for President on August 1, 1979, more than fifteen months before election day, both George Bush and Robert Dole had already been to countless communities seeking votes.

In the presidential campaign, few candidates seeking high office succeeded in winning support through rhetorical skill. Edward M. Kennedy, who galvanized the Democratic National Convention with his address, lost the nomination and John Anderson, whose eloquence won support on college campuses and among voters disillusioned with the two major parties, succeeded only in winning a few votes, on an independent ticket. Others—Ronald Reagan, Walter Mondale, George Bush, and Howard Baker—did demonstrate an ability to speak effectively, but none proved capable of arousing the kind of enthusiasm which Franklin Roosevelt, Adlai Stevenson, and John F. Kennedy had inspired.

Debates among the contenders both during the pre-convention primaries and caucuses and the actual campaign met with mixed success. The candidates displayed a total lack of concern with informing the electorate of their stance on issues, and jockeyed for advantage by agreeing or refusing to engage in debates depending on how participation would affect their election prospects. Initially, incumbent President Jimmy Carter—following the example of Lyndon Johnson in 1964 and Richard Nixon in 1972—refused to debate. Announcing that he would not engage in political campaigning until the hostages in Iran had been released—a posture known as his "Rose Garden strategy"—Carter declined to participate in the September 21 nationally televised debate sponsored by the League of Women Voters, leaving Reagan and Anderson as the participants. Polls indicated that Carter was the loser by his absence and so the President agreed to meet Reagan in a televised debate on October 28, just one week before election day. Whether the exchanges that took place were debates at all or whether they influenced the outcome of the election is difficult to say. The cross-examination format and the questioners with almost no debating background suggest that the confrontations had little in common with a debate. Columnist Nick Thimmesch of the Los Angeles *Times* contended, "The so-called presidential debates are not debates at all, but caricatures of debate, and they never clear the air on issues."

January 1, 1980, marked the beginning of a new decade, and many speakers sought to address the future. This issue of *Representative American Speeches* reflects that interest by including several speeches that explored the challenges, problems, and possible directions to be considered in the next decade in education, the mass media, civil rights, labor, politics, law, and the economy.

In compiling the 1980–1981 edition, this editor has attempted to continue the high standards of his predecessors: A. Craig Baird, 1937–1959; Lester Thonssen, 1960–1969; and Waldo W. Braden, 1970–1980. Readers may notice changes in the current volume, but as the present editor shares the same rhetorical background and philosophy of his predecessors, they are minor. An effort has been made to present a balanced selection of speeches dealing with a variety of subjects that are of interest to the reader, but none should be regarded as endorsements by the editor. In its 44-year history the editors of this series have endeavored to present an impartial, representative selection of addresses that they believe have informed the public or illuminated significant issues. The current editor ascribes to this objective and believes that all of the speeches included in this volume are statements by responsible individuals that are deserving of study.

I thank everyone who helped in the preparation of this volume, particularly Mrs. Janice Anderson, Waldo W. Braden, Stephen L. Cooper, C. David Cornell, Wilbur Samuel Howell, Jean Jackson, Cal M. Logue, Pat Maloney, Harold Mixon, John H. Pennybacker, David Shipley, Lisa Smith, and Joey Tabarlet. I gratefully express special appreciation to Beth Wheeler for her invaluable aid.

OWEN PETERSON

May, 1981
Baton Rouge, Louisiana

THE ELECTION

INAUGURAL ADDRESS[1]

RONALD W. REAGAN[2]

On January 20, 1981, Ronald W. Reagan was sworn in as President of the United States. Louise Sweeney, correspondent for the *Christian Science Monitor*, described the scene:

> The sun broke through right on cue in a blue marble sky for Ronald Reagan as he became 40th President of the United States in one of the most dramatic inaugurations in history. . . . It was a stirring ceremony heightened by the pent-up emotion released when the crowd heard for the first time through an inaugural prayer the news they'd waited so long for: "Thank you, God, for the release of the hostages." . . .
>
> Reagan, looking tanned and fit in the silver-gray tie and morning coat specified for this more formal inauguration took, the 30-second oath of office at 11:57 A.M. Reagan waited for the thunder of a cannon salute to subside before he launched into his inaugural speech, laced with patriotism, firmness, and optimism. He spoke of the "magnificent vista". . . . Stretching before him were thousands of upturned faces, the long tan velvet rug of the mall, the red brick castle of the Smithsonian Institution, the stone spire of the Washington Monument, and, in the misty blue distance, the Lincoln Memorial. . . . The swearing in capped a four-day inaugural celebration—an $11 million extravaganza that . . . included fireworks, constellations of stars, concerts, candlelight suppers, choirs, and satellite balls beamed across the country. (*Christian Science Monitor*, Ja. 21, '81, p 1)

Veteran political observer James Reston characterized the Reagan address as a "theatrical triumph, a cautious compromise between his supporters and opponents at home and abroad." "In his long years as an actor and a politician," Reston asserted, "Ronald Reagan never had such a perfect setting": Everything was

---

[1] Delivered from the west portico of the White House, Washington, D.C., at 12 noon on January 20, 1981.
[2] For biographical note, see Appendix.

planned to perfection for television.... The new President was amiably serious and made one of the best inaugural speeches in recent memory. It was flawlessly presented, and divided into three parts. First, he was courteous to President Carter, thanking him for the transition from one administration to another, but ignoring Carter's successes while emphasizing his failures. Second, he blamed Carter, among others, for the economic distress of the nation.... Yet in the last part of his speech, Mr. Reagan was not only generous but wise and even compassionate.... He has demonstrated in his inaugural address, unlike most politicians these days, that he has the gift of speech. (New York *Times*, Ja. 21, '81, p 31)

Reston's fellow columnist Tom Wicker did not entirely agree, saying that the address seemed rather flat when compared to Reagan's speech accepting the Republican Party nomination. Wicker thought Reagan's address effective only when he played upon "the hackneyed theme of the nation's greatness." Supporting his assertion, Wicker refuted Reagan's claim that the peaceful transfer of authority from the Carter administration to his presidency was "nothing less than a miracle" by citing the routine and frequent peaceful transfer of power from one administration to another in Western Europe and the "miracle" of Canada having pulled off the same transfer twice within the past year. Wicker, however, conceded Reagan's sincerity and noted that "Many Americans needed reassurance, renewed faith, their confidence restored." (New York *Times*, Ja. 23, '81, p 23)

William Safire, who at one time was a speechwriter for Richard Nixon, thought that Reagan gave two speeches. "The first was an FDR-style warning of economic peril, coupled with an attack on big Government as the source of our problem." In the second speech, begun about halfway through according to Safire, Reagan "resurrected the 'forgotten American' and evoked memories of patriotic fervor, national will, and individual sacrifice." Safire revealed that speech writers Ken Khachigian, Anthony Dolan, and Richard Moore assisted in the preparation of the address and credited Moore with a "stroke of genius" in suggesting that the inaugural face westward and having Reagan point out the monuments in front of him. According to Safire, Reagan instructed his writers to consult with Vernon Jordan of the Urban League, an organization not sympathetic to Reagan's candidacy, on some passages. Reagan's speech, in Safire's opinion, was "serious rather than profound, moving rather than inspiring. The inaugural address was the product of his own mind and his own life: what we heard is what we get. Churchill he is not, but Reagan he really is." (New York *Times*, Ja. 22, '81, p 23)

The New York *Times*, in an editorial, observed:

> Words, particularly inaugural words, often haunt the Presidents who speak them. They represent no achievement, only aspiration. With his first words on the greatest stage of all, Ronald Reagan left the impression that he aspires to lead not a revolution but a revival, not a global crusade but an inspiring diplomacy. (New York *Times*, Ja. 21, '81, p 30)

Readers of this speech and students of public address trying to assess its effectiveness in the future must always keep in mind that a second unprecedented drama, which threatened to overshadow the inauguration, was being played out at the same time. After a 14-month traumatic ordeal, the American hostages in Iran had been released. Harvard historian Frank Friedel described the situation as follows: "This is the only time a twin star, or binary event, has occurred at an inauguration. I can't think of any parallel." Indeed, the events related to the release of the hostages to a considerable extent overshadowed the inauguration in the coverage by the media and in the emotions of Americans. Any attempt to assess the effectiveness of Ronald Reagan's inaugural address must take into account this twin drama.

Thank you Senator Hatfield, Mr. Chief Justice, Mr. President, Vice President Bush, Vice President Mondale, Senator Baker, Speaker O'Neill, Reverend Moomaw, and my fellow citizens.

To a few of us here today this is a solemn and most momentous occasion. And, yet, in the history of our nation it is a commonplace occurrence. The orderly transfer of authority as called for in the Constitution routinely takes place, as it has for almost two centuries, and few of us stop to think how unique we really are. In the eyes of many in the world, this every-four-year ceremony we accept as normal is nothing less than a miracle.

Mr. President, I want our fellow citizens to know how much you did to carry on this tradition. By your gracious cooperation in the transition process you have shown a watching world that we are a united people pledged to maintaining a political system which guarantees individual liberty to a greater degree than any other, and I thank you and your people for all your help in maintaining the continuity which is the bulwark of our republic.

The business of our nation goes forward. These United States are confronted with an economic affliction of great proportions. We suffer from the longest and one of the worst sustained inflations in our national history. It distorts our economic decisions, penalizes thrift, and crushes the struggling young and the fixed-income elderly alike. It threatens to shatter the lives of millions of our people.

Idle industries have cast workers into unemployment, human misery, and personal indignity. Those who do work are denied a fair return for their labor by a tax system which penalizes successful achievement and keeps us from maintaining full productivity.

But great as our tax burden is, it has not kept pace with public spending. For decades we have piled deficit upon deficit, mortgaging our future and our children's future for the temporary convenience of the present. To continue this long trend is to guarantee tremendous social, cultural, political, and economic upheavals.

You and I, as individuals, can, by borrowing, live beyond our means, but for only a limited period of time. Why, then, should we think that collectively, as a nation, we're not bound by that same limitation? We must act today in order to preserve tomorrow. And let there be no misunderstanding—we are going to begin to act, beginning today.

The economic ills we suffer have come upon us over several decades. They will not go away in days, weeks, or months, but they will go away. They will go away because we as Americans have the capacity now, as we've had in the past, to do whatever needs to be done to preserve this last and greatest bastion of freedom.

In this present crisis, government is not the solution to our problem; government is the problem. From time to time we've been tempted to believe that society has become too complex to be managed by self-rule, that government by an elite group is superior to government for, by, and of the people. But, if no one among us is capable of governing himself, then who among us has the capacity to govern someone else? All of us together—in and out of government—must bear the burden. The solutions we seek must be equitable with no one group singled out to pay a higher price.

We hear much of special interest groups. Well, our concern must be for a special interest group that has been too long neglected. It knows no sectional boundaries or ethnic and racial divisions, and it crosses political party lines. It is made up of men and women who raise our food, patrol our streets, man our mines and factories, teach our children, keep our homes, and heal us when we're sick—professionals, industrialists, shopkeepers, clerks, cabbies, and truckdrivers. They are, in short, "We the people," this breed called Americans.

Well, this administration's objective will be a healthy, vigorous, growing economy that provides equal opportunities for all Americans with no barriers born of bigotry or discrimination. Putting America back to work means putting all Americans back to work. Ending inflation means freeing all Americans from the terror of runaway living costs. All must share in the productive work of this "new beginning," and all must share in the bounty of a revived economy. With the idealism and fair play which are the core of our system and our strength, we can have a strong and prosperous America, at peace with itself and the world.

So, as we begin, let us take inventory. We are a nation that has a government—not the other way around. And this makes us special among the nations of the earth. Our government has no power except that granted it by the people. It is time to check and reverse the growth of government which shows signs of having grown beyond the consent of the governed.

It is my intention to curb the size and influence of the Federal establishment and to demand recognition of the distinction between the powers granted to the Federal Government and those reserved to the states or to the people. All of us need—all of us to be reminded that the Federal Government did not create the states; the states created the Federal Government.

Now, so there will be no misunderstanding, it's not my intention to do away with government. It is rather to make it work—work with us, not over us; to stand by our side, not ride on our back. Government can and must provide opportunity, not smother it; foster productivity, not stifle it.

If we look to the answer as to why for so many years we achieved so much, prospered as no other people on earth, it was because here in this land we unleashed the energy and individual genius of man to a greater extent than has ever been done before. Freedom and the dignity of the individual have been more available and assured here than in any other place on earth. The price for this freedom at times has been high. But we have never been unwilling to pay that price.

It is no coincidence that our present troubles parallel and are proportionate to the intervention and intrusion in our lives that result from unnecessary and excessive growth of government. It is time for us to realize that we're too great a nation to limit ourselves to small dreams. We're not, as some would have us believe, doomed to an inevitable decline. I do not believe in a fate that will fall on us no matter what we do. I do believe in a fate that will fall on us if we do nothing. So, with all the creative energy at our command, let us begin an era of national renewal. Let us renew our determination, our courage, and our strength. And let us renew our faith and our hope.

We have every right to dream heroic dreams. Those who say that we're in a time when there are no heroes, they just don't know where to look. You can see heroes every day going in and out of factory gates. Others, a handful in number, produce enough food to feed all of us and then the world beyond. You meet heroes across a counter. And they're on both sides of that counter. There are entrepreneurs with faith in themselves and faith in an idea who create new jobs, new wealth and opportunity. They're individuals and families whose taxes support the government and whose voluntary gifts support church, charity, culture, art, and education. Their patriotism is quiet but deep. Their values sustain our national life.

Now, I have used the words "they" and "their" in speaking of these heroes. I could say "you" and "your," because I'm addressing the heroes of whom I speak—you, the citizens of this blessed land. Your dreams, your hopes, your goals are going to be the dreams, the hopes, and the goals of this administration, so help me God.

We shall reflect the compassion that is so much a part of your makeup. How can we love our country and not love our countrymen; and loving them, reach out a hand when they fall, heal them when they're sick, and provide opportunity to make them self-sufficient so they will be equal in fact and not just in theory?

Can we solve the problems confronting us? Well, the answer is an unequivocal and emphatic "yes." To paraphrase Winston Churchill, I did not take the oath I've just taken with the intention of presiding over the dissolution of the world's strongest economy.

In the days ahead I will propose removing the roadblocks that have slowed our economy and reduced productivity. Steps will be taken aimed at restoring the balance between the various levels of government. Progress may be slow, measured in inches and feet, not miles, but we will progress. It is time to reawaken this industrial giant, to get government back within its means, and to lighten our punitive tax burden. And these will be our first priorities, and on these principles there will be no compromise.

On the eve of our struggle for independence a man who might have been one of the greatest among the Founding Fathers, Dr. Joseph Warren, president of the Massachusetts Congress, said to his fellow Americans, "Our country is in danger, but not to be despaired of. . . . On you depend the fortunes of America. You are to decide the important question upon which rests the happiness and the liberty of millions yet unborn. Act worthy of yourselves."

Well, I believe we, the Americans of today, are ready to

act worthy of ourselves, ready to do what must be done to ensure happiness and liberty for ourselves, our children, and our children's children. And as we renew ourselves here in our own land, we will be seen as having greater strength throughout the world. We will again be the exemplar of freedom and a beacon of hope for those who do not now have freedom.

To those neighbors and allies who share our freedom, we will strengthen our historic ties and assure them of our support and firm commitment. We will match loyalty with loyalty. We will strive for mutually beneficial relations. We will not use our friendship to impose on their sovereignty, for our own sovereignty is not for sale.

As for the enemies of freedom, those who are potential adversaries, they will be reminded that peace is the highest aspiration of the American people. We will negotiate for it, sacrifice for it; we will not surrender for it now or ever.

Our forbearance should never be misunderstood. Our reluctance for conflict should not be misjudged as a failure of will. When action is required to preserve our national security, we will act. We will maintain sufficient strength to prevail if need be, knowing that if we do so we have the best chance of never having to use that strength.

Above all we must realize that no arsenal or no weapon in the arsenals of the world is so formidable as the will and moral courage of free men and women. It is a weapon our adversaries in today's world do not have. It is a weapon that we as Americans do have. Let that be understood by those who practice terrorism and prey upon their neighbors.

I'm told that tens of thousands of prayer meetings are being held on this day; for that I'm deeply grateful. We are a nation under God, and I believe God intended for us to be free. It would be fitting and good, I think, if on each Inaugural Day in future years it should be declared a day of prayer.

This is the first time in our history that this ceremony has been held, as you've been told, on this West Front of the Capitol. Standing here, one faces a magnificent vista, opening up on this city's special beauty and history. At the end of this open mall are those shrines to the giants on whose shoulders we stand.

Directly in front of me, the monument to a monumental man, George Washington, father of our country. A man of humility who came to greatness reluctantly. He led America out of revolutionary victory into infant nationhood. Off to one side, the stately memorial to Thomas Jefferson. The Declaration of Independence flames with his eloquence. And then, beyond the Reflecting Pool, the dignified columns of the Lincoln Memorial. Whoever would understand in his heart the meaning of America will find it in the life of Abraham Lincoln.

Beyond those monuments to heroism is the Potomac River, and on the far shore the sloping hills of Arlington National Cemetery, with its row upon row of simple white markers bearing crosses or Stars of David. They add up to only a tiny fraction of the price that has been paid for our freedom.

Each one of those markers is a monument to the kind of hero I spoke of earlier. Their lives ended in places called Belleau Wood, The Argonne, Omaha Beach, Salerno, and halfway around the world on Guadalcanal, Tarawa, Pork Chop Hill, the Chosin Reservoir, and in a hundred rice paddies and jungles of a place called Vietnam.

Under one such marker lies a young man, Martin Treptow, who left his job in a small town barbershop in 1917 to go to France with the famed Rainbow Division. There, on the western front, he was killed trying to carry a message between battalions under heavy artillery fire.

We're told that on his body was found a diary. On the flyleaf under the heading, "My Pledge," he had written these words: "America must win this war. Therefore I will work, I will save, I will sacrifice, I will endure, I will fight cheerfully and do my utmost, as if the issue of the whole struggle depended on me alone."

The crisis we are facing today does not require of us the kind of sacrifice that Martin Treptow and so many thousands of others were called upon to make. It does require, however, our best effort and our willingness to believe in ourselves and

to believe in our capacity to perform great deeds, to believe
that together with God's help we can and will resolve the
problems which now confront us.

And after all, why shouldn't we believe that? We are
Americans.

God bless you, and thank you.

FAREWELL ADDRESS[1]

JIMMY CARTER[2]

Seated in front of his desk in the Oval Office in the White
House on the evening of January 14, 1981, Jimmy Carter addressed
the American people for the last time as President of the United
States. Carried by all three commercial networks and public television, the President's 17-minute farewell address was viewed by
millions.

Realizing that this probably was his final opportunity to make
a lasting, perhaps historic, impression on a vast television audience, President Carter took great pains in the preparation of the
address. The speech, according to Terence Smith (New York
Times, Ja. 15, '81), was a product of weeks of drafting and redraft-
ing. Mr. Carter himself wrote the first outline and then reworked
drafts provided by speechwriters Hendrik Hertzberg and Gordon
Stewart. Communications consultant Gerald Rafshoon and poll-
ster Patrick H. Caddell also contributed to the final version, which
was completed late in the afternoon of the day of its delivery.

Tom Wicker of the New York *Times* (Ja. 16, '81) described the
speech: "President Carter's farewell address became him well. He
offered best wishes to the man who defeated him," although never
mentioning him by name, "reminded the nation of its enduring
values, and made a modest final appeal for the goals that had most
engaged him." The departing President included no mention of
the economy, one of the key problems that had made him a one-
term President, and spoke only briefly of the American hostages
whose captivity in Iran haunted his last year in office. In the ad-

[1] Delivered from the Oval Office of the White House, Washington, D.C., 8 P.M.,
January 14, 1981.
[2] For biographical note, see Appendix.

dress, Carter seemed more concerned with the future than with the present or past. He also seemed to be trying to define himself on those issues that mattered most to him. His emphasis on the threat of a nuclear holocaust suggests that he wanted to be remembered for his efforts to reduce that risk as well as to establish a tough new standard by which to measure his successor.

The speech was described by reporters as "in quiet, low-key style," "sombre," "a low-keyed but deeply felt farewell speech," a "brief but poignant address," notable for Carter's "characteristic absence of purple passages," "sermon-like," "modest," "reflective," "relaxed, low-key," "graceful," and "at times moving." One observer labeled him the "preacher-president."

The address, in the opinion of Charles Krauthammer of the *New Republic* (Ja. 31, '81), was "carefully designed to fit the farewell format. It was a final I-told-you-so meant for rereading in a decade. . . . Carter's speech, intended for the future, revealed what for years we had been clamoring for—his vision of the present." Richard Strout [*Christian Science Monitor*, Ja. 16, '81] believed that many of the millions of viewers were "moved in spite of themselves by Carter's quiet dignity." Columnist William Safire (New York *Times Magazine*, F. 1, '81) chose the last sentence as the high point of the address. "Not since Lincoln's speech at Springfield had we heard a man elected President end a farewell address properly. 'Thank you fellow citizens,' said Mr. Carter, 'and farewell.' "

Good evening. In a few days, I will lay down my official responsibilities in this office to take up once more the only title in our democracy superior to that of President, the title of citizen.

Of Vice President Mondale, my Cabinet and the hundreds of others who have served with me during these four years, I wish to say publicly what I have said in private. I thank them for the dedication and competence they have brought to the service of our country.

But I owe my deepest thanks to you, the American people, because you gave me this extraordinary opportunity to serve. We have faced great challenges together. We know that future problems will also be difficult, but I am now more convinced than ever that the United States—better than any other nation—can meet successfully whatever the future might bring.

These last four years have made me more certain than ever of the inner strength of our country—the unchanging value of our principles and ideals, the stability of our political system, the ingenuity and decency of our people.

Tonight I would like first to say a few words about this most special office, the Presidency of the United States.

This is at once the most powerful office in the world—and among the most severely constrained by law and custom. The President is given a broad responsibility to lead—but cannot do so without the support and consent of the people, expressed formally through the Congress and informally through a whole range of public and private institutions.

This is as it should be. Within our system of government every American has a right and duty to help shape the future course of the United States. Thoughtful criticism and close scrutiny of all government officials by the press and the public are an important part of our democratic society. Now as in our past, only the understanding and involvement of the people through full and open debate can help to avoid mistakes and assure the continued dignity and safety of the nation.

Today we are asking our political system to do things of which the founding fathers never dreamed. The government they designed for a few hundred thousand people now serves a nation of almost 230 million people. Their small coastal republic now spans beyond a continent, and we now have the responsibility to help lead much of the world through difficult times to a secure and prosperous future.

Today, as people have become more doubtful of the ability of the government to deal with our problems, we are increasingly drawn to single-issue groups and special interest organizations to insure that whatever else happens our own personal views and our own private interests are protected. This is a disturbing factor in American political life. It tends to distort our purposes because the national interest is not always the sum of all our single or special interests. We are all Americans together and we must not forget that the common good is our common interest and our individual responsibility.

Because of the fragmented pressures of special interests, it is very important that the office of the President be a strong one, and that its constitutional authority be preserved. The President is the only elected official charged with representing all the people. In the moments of decision, after the different and conflicting views have been aired, it is the President who then must speak to the nation and for the nation.

I understand, as few others can, how formidable is the task the President-elect is about to undertake. To the very limits of conscience and conviction, I pledge to support him in that task. I wish him success and Godspeed.

I know from experience that Presidents have to face major issues that are controversial, broad in scope, and which do not arouse the natural support of a political majority.

For a few minutes now, I want to lay aside my role as a leader of one nation and speak to you as a fellow citizen of the world about three such issues: The threat of nuclear destruction, our stewardship of the physical resources of our planet and the pre-eminence of the basic rights of human beings.

It has now been 35 years since the first atomic bomb fell on Hiroshima. The great majority of the world's people cannot remember a time when the nuclear shadow did not hang over the earth. Our minds have adjusted to it, as after a time our eyes adjust to the dark.

Yet the risk of a nuclear conflagration has not lessened. It has not happened yet, but that can give us little comfort—for it only has to happen once.

The danger is becoming greater. As the arsenals of the super powers grow in size and sophistication and as other governments acquire these weapons, it may only be a matter of time before madness, desperation, greed or miscalculation lets loose this terrible force.

In an all-out nuclear war, more destructive power than in all of World War II would be unleashed every second for the long afternoon it would take for all the missiles and bombs to fall. A World War II every second—more people killed in the first few hours than all the wars of history put together. The survivors, if any, would live in despair amid the poisoned ruins of a civilization that had committed suicide.

National weakness—real or perceived—can tempt aggression and thus cause war. That is why the United States cannot neglect its military strength. We must and we will remain strong. But with equal determination, the United States and all countries must find ways to control and reduce the horrifying danger that is posed by the world's stockpiles of nuclear arms.

This has been a concern of every American President since the moment we first saw what these weapons could do. Our leaders will require our understanding and support as they grapple with this difficult but crucial challenge. There is no disagreement on the goals or the basic approach to controlling this enormous destructive force. The answer lies not just in the attitudes or actions of world leaders, but in the concern and demands of all of us as we continue our struggle to preserve the peace.

Nuclear weapons are an expression of one side of our human character. But there is another side. The same rocket technology that delivers nuclear warheads has also taken us peacefully into space. From that perspective, we see our earth as it really is—a small and fragile and beautiful blue globe, the only home we have. We see no barriers of race or religion or country. We see the essential unity of our species and our planet; and with faith and common sense that bright vision will utimately prevail.

Another major challenge is to protect the quality of this world within which we live. The shadows that fall across the future are cast not only by the kinds of weapons we have built but by the kind of world we will either nourish or neglect. There are real and growing dangers to our simple and most precious possessions: the air we breathe, the water we drink and the land which sustains us. The rapid depletion of irreplaceable minerals, the erosion of topsoil, the destruction of beauty, the blight of pollution, the demands of increasing billions of people all combine to create problems which are easy to observe and predict but difficult to resolve. If we do not act, the world of the year 2000 will be much less able to sustain life than it is now.

But there is no reason for despair. Acknowledging the

physical realities of our planet does not mean a dismal future of endless sacrifice. In fact, acknowledging these realities is the first step in dealing with them. We can meet the resource problems of the world—water, food, minerals, farmlands, forests, overpopulation, pollution—if we tackle them with courage and foresight.

I have just been talking about forces of potential destruction that mankind has developed and how we might control them. It is equally important that we remember the beneficial forces that we have evolved over the ages and hold fast to them.

One of those constructive forces is enhancement of individual human freedoms through the strengthening of democracy, and the fight against deprivation, torture, terrorism and the persecution of people throughout the world. The struggle for human rights overrides all differences of color, nation or language.

Those who hunger for freedom, who thirst for human dignity, and who suffer for the sake of justice—they are the patriots of this cause.

I believe will all my heart that America must always stand for these basic human rights—at home and abroad. That is both our history and our destiny.

America did not invent human rights. In a very real sense it is the other way around. Human rights invented America.

Ours was the first nation in the history of the world to be founded explicitly on such an idea. Our social and political progress has been based on one fundamental principle—the value and importance of the individual. The fundamental force that unites us is not kinship or place of origin or religious preference. The love of liberty is the common blood that flows in our American veins.

The battle for human rights—at home and abroad—is far from over. We should never be surprised nor discouraged because the impact of our efforts has had varied results. Rather we should take pride that the ideals which gave birth to our nation still inspire the hopes of oppressed people around the world. We have no cause for self-righteousness or complacency. But we have every reason to persevere, both in our own country and beyond our borders.

If we are to serve as a beacon for human rights we must continue to perfect here at home the rights and values we espouse around the world: A decent education for our children, adequate medical care for all Americans, an end to discrimination against minorities and women, a job for those able to work and freedom from injustice and religious intolerance.

We live in a time of transition, an uneasy era which is likely to endure for the rest of this century. It will be a period of tensions both within nations and between nations—of competition for scarce resources, of social, political and economic stresses and strains. During this period we may be tempted to abandon some of the time-honored principles and commitments which have been proven during the difficult times of past generations.

We must never yield to this temptation. Our American values are not luxuries but necessities—not the salt in our bread but the bread itself. Our common vision of a free and just society is our greatest source of cohesion at home and strength abroad—greater even than the bounty of our material blessings.

Remember these words. "We hold these truths to be self-evident, that all men are created equal; that they are endowed by their creator with certain inalienable rights; that among these are life, liberty and the pursuit of happiness."

This vision still grips the imagination of the world. But we know that democracy is always an unfinished creation. Each generation must renew its foundations. Each generation must rediscover the meaning of this hallowed vision in the light of its own modern challenges. For this generation, life is nuclear survival; liberty is human rights; the pursuit of happiness is a planet whose resources are devoted to the physical and spiritual nourishment of its inhabitants.

As I return home to the South where I was born and raised, I am looking forward to the opportunity to reflect and further to assess—I hope with accuracy—the circumstances of our times. I intend to give our new President my support, and I intend to work as a citizen, as I have worked as President, for the values this nation was founded to secure.

Again, from the bottom of my heart, I want to express to you the gratitude I feel. Thank you, fellow citizens, and farewell. (New York *Times,* Ja. 15, '81, p 12)

THE DREAM SHALL NEVER DIE:
SPEECH TO THE DEMOCRATIC NATIONAL CONVENTION[1]

EDWARD M. KENNEDY[2]

As often happens when an incumbent President is assured of renomination, the 1980 Democratic national convention was a lack-lustre affair at the outset. Although a Harris poll rated his national support at only 22 percent, President Jimmy Carter had won enough primaries and delegates to guarantee his candidacy. The only threat to renomination lay in the attempt of Senator Edward M. Kennedy of Massachusetts, his main challenger, to change the convention rules and secure release of committed delegates. When Kennedy lost the rules fight, he congratulated the President and announced his decision to withdraw from the contest.

Kennedy, however, had decided a week earlier that regardless of the outcome on the rules challenge he would speak to the convention in support of four platform planks he proposed—the first candidate to do so since William Jennings Bryan made his famous Cross of Gold speech in 1896. Kennedy's speechwriters, who for weeks had been reading memorable convention addresses and scrutinizing Reagan's record, prepared a draft which the senator tested at several delegate caucuses. Ted Sorenson, a John F. Kennedy speechwriter, submitted stylistic changes and Arthur Schlesinger offered suggestions. With a final draft in hand, Kennedy

---

[1] Delivered to the Democratic National Convention, Madison Square Garden, New York, Tuesday evening, August 12, 1980.
[2] For biographical note, see Appendix.

began practicing on a Teleprompter set up in his hotel suite two
days before he delivered the speech.

The speech, most observers agreed, transformed political defeat into emotional victory. Reporters described it as "rousing,"
"memorable," "powerful," "graceful," "passionate," and "eloquent." President Carter, in his acceptance speech, called it a
"magnificent statement of what the Democratic Party has meant
to the people of this country." The press reported that the speech
"galvanized" and "electrified" the convention. Louis Heren of *The
Times* (London) wrote that "many a hardened politician wept that
night." The *Telegraph* (London) correspondent observed, "Carter
won the nomination. . . . Kennedy won the applause and the heart
of the convention." The *Standard* (London) labeled the Kennedy
address as "the speech of his life" and described it as "a moment of
genuine passion" in a convention lacking in drama and excitement. *Newsweek* called the speech a "barnburner" and "Kennedy's best."

Newsweek perhaps best described the reaction to Kennedy's
speech:

> The crowd's response was very nearly cathartic after so
> many months of bitter rivalry. . . . For 39 uninterrupted min-
> utes, the yearning crowd packed into Madison Square Garden
> last Tuesday night cheered, chanted, and cried for the man
> who would not be king—at least for this year. . . . "We want
> Ted!" they roared back, over and over again. It was an unpre-
> cedented moment in American politics, the spectacle of a failed
> candidate galvanizing his party's national convention and
> overshadowing a President who was about to be renominated.
> Kennedy may have lost the nomination, but . . . that was
> the only thing he lost. In one night, with one superb speech he
> was by turns graceful, rousing, poetic, and defiant. Kennedy
> transformed what was supposed to have been a tearful last
> hurrah into a triumphant call to arms and he emerged as a
> more potent political figure than at any point in his frustrated
> pursuit of the nomination. (*Newsweek*, Ag. 25, '80, p 31)

Kennedy delivered the speech at the August 12, 1980, evening
session of the Democratic National Convention, held in Madison
Square Garden in New York City.

Well, things worked out a little different than I thought,
but let me tell you, I still love New York.

My fellow Democrats and my fellow Americans: I have

come here tonight not to argue for a candidacy, but to affirm a cause.

I am asking you to renew the commitment of the Democratic Party to economic justice. I am asking you to renew our commitment to a fair and lasting prosperity that can put America back to work.

This is the cause that brought me into the campaign and that sustained me for nine months, across a hundred thousand miles, in forty different states. We had our losses, but the pain of our defeats is far, far less than the pain of the people I have met. We have learned that it is important to take issues seriously, but never to take ourselves too seriously.

The serious issue before us tonight is the cause for which the Democratic Party has stood in its finest hours—the cause that keeps our party young—and makes it, in the second century of its age, the largest political party in this Republic and the longest lasting political party on this planet.

Our cause has been since the days of Thomas Jefferson, the cause of the common man—and the common woman. Our commitment has been, since the days of Andrew Jackson, to all those he called "the humble members of society—the farmers, mechanics, and laborers." On this foundation, we have defined our values, refined our policies, and refreshed our faith.

Now I take the unusual step of carrying the cause and the commitment of my campaign personally to our national convention. I speak out of a deep sense of urgency about the anguish and anxiety I have seen across America. I speak out of deep belief in the ideals of the Democratic Party, and in the potential of that party and of a President to make a difference. I speak out of a deep trust in our capacity to proceed with boldness and a common vision that will feel and heal the suffering of our time—and the division of our party.

The economic plank of this platform on its face concerns only material things; but is also a moral issue that I raise tonight. It has taken many forms over many years. In this campaign, and in this country that we seek to lead, the challenge in 1980 is to give our voice and our vote for these fundamental Democratic principles:

Let us pledge that we will never misuse unemployment, high interest rates, and human misery as false weapons against inflation.

Let us pledge that employment will be the first priority of our economic policy.

Let us pledge that there will be security for all who are now at work. Let us pledge that there will be jobs for all who are out of work—and we will not compromise on the issue of jobs.

These are not simplistic pledges. Simply put, they are the heart of our tradition; they have been the soul of our party across the generations. It is the glory and the greatness of our tradition to speak for those who have no voice, to remember those who are forgotten, to respond to the frustrations and fulfill the aspirations of all Americans seeking a better life in a better land.

We dare not forsake that tradition. We cannot let the great purposes of the Democratic Party become the bygone passages of history. We must not permit the Republicans to seize and run on the slogans of prosperity.

We heard the orators at their convention all trying to talk like Democrats. They proved that even Republican nominees can quote Franklin Roosevelt to their own purpose. The Grand Old Party thinks it has found a great new trick. But forty years ago, an earlier generation of Republicans attempted that same trick. And Franklin Roosevelt himself replied "Most Republican leaders . . . have bitterly fought and blocked the forward surge of average men and women in their pursuit of happiness. Let us not be deluded that overnight those leaders have suddenly become the friends of average men and women. . . . You know, very few of us are that gullible."

And four years later, when the Republicans tried that trick again, Franklin Roosevelt asked: "Can the Ole Guard pass itself off as the New Deal? I think not. We have all seen many marvelous stunts in the circus—but no performing elephant could turn a handspring without falling flat on its back."

The 1980 Republican convention was awash with croco-
dile tears for our economic distress but it is by their long
record and not their recent words that you shall know them.

The same Republicans who are talking about the crisis of
unemployment have nominated a man who once said—and I
quote: "Unemployment insurance is a prepaid vacation plan
for freeloaders." And that nominee is no friend of labor.

The same Republicans who are talking about the problems of the inner cities have nominated a man who said—and
I quote: "I have included in my morning and evening prayers
everyday the prayer that the federal government not bail out
New York." And that nominee is no friend of this city and of
our great urban centers.

The same Republicans who are talking about security for
the elderly have nominated a man who said just four years
ago that participation in Social Security "should be made voluntary." And that nominee is no friend of the senior citizen.

The same Republicans who are talking about preserving
the environment have nominated a man who last year made
the preposterous statement, and I quote: "Eighty percent of
air pollution comes from plants and trees." And that nominee
is no friend of the environment.

And the same Republicans who are invoking Franklin
Roosevelt have nominated a man who said in 1976—and
these are his exact words: "Fascism was really the basis of the
New Deal." And that nominee, whose name is Ronald Reagan, has no right to quote Franklin Delano Roosevelt.

The great adventure which our opponents offer is a voy-
age into the past. Progress is our heritage, not theirs. What is
right for us as Democrats is also the right way for Democrats
to win.

The commitment I seek is not to outworn views, but to
old values that will never wear out. Programs may sometimes
become obsolete, but the ideal of fairness always endures.
Circumstances may change, but the work of compassion must
continue. It is surely correct that we cannot solve problems
by throwing money at them; but it is also correct that we dare
not throw our national problems into a scrap heap of inatten-

tion and indifference. The poor may be out of political fashion, but they are not without human needs. The middle-class may be angry, but they have not lost the dream that all Americans can advance together.

The demand of our people in 1980 is not for smaller government or bigger government, but for better government. Some say that government is always bad, and that spending for basic social programs is the root of our economic evils. But we reply, The present inflation and recession cost our economy $200 billion a year. We reply, Inflation and unemployment are the biggest spenders of all.

The task of leadership in 1980 is not to parade scapegoats or to seek refuge in reaction but to match our power to the possibilities of progress.

While others talked of free enterprise, it was the Democratic Party that acted—and we ended excessive regulation in the airline and trucking industry. We restored competition to the marketplace. And I take some satisfaction that this deregulation was legislation that I sponsored and passed in the Congress of the United States.

As Democrats, we recognize that each generation of Americans has a rendezvous with a different reality. The answers of one generation become the questions of the next generation. But there is a guiding star in the American firmament. It is as old as the revolutionary belief that all people are created equal—and as clear as the contemporary condition of Liberty City and the South Bronx. Again and again, Democratic leaders have followed that star—and they have given new meaning to the old values of liberty and justice for all.

We are the party of the New Freedom, the New Deal, and the New Frontier. We have always been the party of hope. So this year, let us offer new hope—new hope to an America uncertain about the present, but unsurpassed in its potential for the future.

To all those who are idle in the cities and industries of America, let us provide new hope for the dignity of useful work. Democrats have always believed that a basic civil right of all Americans is the right to earn their own way. The party of the people must always be the party of full employment.

To all those who doubt the future of our economy, let us provide new hope for the reindustrialization of America. Let our vision reach beyond the next election or the next year to a new generation of prosperity. If we could rebuild Germany and Japan after World War II, then surely we can reindustrialize our own nation and revive our inner cities in the 1980s.

To all those who work hard for a living wage, let us provide new hope that the price of their employment shall not be an unsafe workplace and death at an earlier age.

To all those who inhabit our land, from California to the New York island, from the Redwood forest to the Gulfstream waters, let us provide new hope that prosperity shall not be purchased by poisoning the air, the rivers and the natural resources that are the greatest gift of this continent. We must insist that our children and grandchildren shall inherit a land which they can truly call America the beautiful.

To all those who see the worth of their work and their savings taken by inflation, let us offer new hope for a stable economy. We must meet the pressures of the present by invoking the full power of government to master increasing prices. In candor, we must say that the federal budget can be balanced only by policies that bring us to a balanced prosperity of full employment and price restraint.

And to all those overburdened by an unfair tax structure, let us provide new hope for real tax reform. Instead of shutting down classrooms, let us shut off tax shelters.

Instead of cutting out school lunches, let us cut off tax subsidies for expensive business lunches that are nothing more than food stamps for the rich.

The tax cut of our Republican opponents takes the name of tax reform in vain. It is a wonderfully Republican idea that would redistribute income in the wrong direction. It is good news for any of you with incomes over $200,000 a year. For the few of you, it offers a pot of gold worth $14,000. But the Republican tax cut is bad news for middle income families. For the many of you, they plan a pittance of $200 a year. And that is not what the Democratic Party means when we say tax reform.

The vast majority of Americans cannot afford this panacea from a Republican nominee who has denounced the progressive income tax as the invention of Karl Marx. I am afraid he has confused Karl Marx with Theodore Roosevelt, that obscure Republican President who sought and fought for a tax system based on ability to pay. Theodore Roosevelt was not Karl Marx—and the Republican tax scheme is not tax reform.

Finally, we cannot have a fair prosperity in isolation from a fair society.

So I will continue to stand for national health insurance. We must not surrender to the relentless medical inflation that can bankrupt almost anyone—and that may soon break the budgets of government at every level.

Let us insist on real controls over what doctors and hospitals can charge. Let us resolve that the state of a family's health shall never depend on the size of a family's wealth.

The President, the vice president, and the members of Congress have a medical plan that meets their needs in full. Whenever senators and representatives catch a little cold, the Capitol physician will see them immediately, treat them promptly, and fill a prescription on the spot. We do not get a bill even if we ask for it. And when do you think was the last time a member of Congress asked for a bill from the federal government?

I say again, as I have said before: if health insurance is good enough for the President, the vice president, and the Congress of the United States, then it is good enough for all of you and for every family in America.

There were some who said we should be silent about our differences on issues during this convention. But the heritage of the Democratic Party has been a history of democracy. We fight hard because we care deeply about our principles and purposes. We did not flee this struggle. And we welcome this contrast with the empty and expedient spectacle last month in Detroit where no nomination was contested, no question was debated and no one dared to raise any doubt or dissent.

Democrats can be proud that we chose a different course—and a different platform.

We can be proud that our party stands for investment in safe energy instead of a nuclear future that may threaten the future itself. We must not permit the neighborhoods of America to be permanently shadowed by the fear of another Three Mile Island.

We can be proud that our party stands for a fair housing law to unlock the doors of discrimination once and for all. The American house will be divided against itself so long as there is prejudice against any American family buying or renting a home.

And we can be proud that our party stands plainly, publicly, and persistently for the ratification of the Equal Rights Amendment. Women hold their rightful place at our convention; and women must have their rightful place in the Constitution of the United States. On this issue, we will not yield, we will not equivocate, we will not rationalize, explain, or excuse. We will stand for E.R.A. and for the recognition at long last that our nation had not only founding fathers, but founding mothers as well.

A fair prosperity and a just society are within our vision and our grasp. We do not have every answer. There are questions not yet asked, waiting for us in the recesses of the future.

But of this much we can be certain, because it is the lesson of all our history:

Together a President and the people can make a difference. I have found that faith still alive wherever I have traveled across the land. So let us reject the counsel of retreat and the call to reaction. Let us go forward in the knowledge that history only helps those who help themselves.

There will be setbacks and sacrifices in the years ahead. But I am convinced that we as a people are ready to give something back to our country in return for all it has given us. Let this be our commitment: Whatever sacrifices must be made will be shared—and shared fairly. And let this be our confidence at the end of our journey and always before us shines that ideal of liberty and justice for all.

In closing, let me say a few words to all those I have met and all those who have supported me at this convention and across the country.

There were hard hours on our journey. Often we sailed against the wind, but always we kept our rudder true. There were so many of you who stayed the course and shared our hope. You gave your help; but even more, you gave your hearts. Because of you, this has been a happy campaign. You welcomed Joan and me and our family into your homes and neighborhoods, your churches, your campuses, and your union halls. When I think back on all the memories, I think of you. I recall the poet's words, and I say: "What golden friends I had."

Among you, my golden friends across this land, I have listened and learned.

I have listened to Kenny Dubois, a glassblower in Charleston, West Virginia, who has ten children to support, but has lost his job after 35 years, just three years short of qualifying for his pension.

I have listened to the Trachta family, who farm in Iowa and who wonder whether they can pass the good life and the good earth on to their children.

I have listened to a grandmother in East Oakland, who no longer has a phone to call her grandchildren, because she gave it up to pay the rent on her small apartment.

I have listened to young workers out of work, to students without the tuition for college, and to families without the chance to own a home. I have seen the closed factories and the stalled assembly lines of Anderson, Indiana and South Gate, California. I have seen too many—far too many—idle men and women desperate to work. I have seen too many—far too many—working families desperate to protect the value of their wages from the ravages of inflation.

Yet I have also sensed a yearning for new hope among the people in every state where I have seen. I felt it in their handshakes; I saw it in their faces. I shall never forget the mothers who carried children to our rallies. I shall always remember the elderly who have lived in an America of high purpose and who believe it can all happen again.

Tonight, in their name, I have come here to speak for them. For their sake, I ask you to stand with them. On their behalf, I ask you to restate and reaffirm the timeless truth of our party.

I congratulate President Carter on his victory here. I am confident that the Democratic Party will reunite on the basis of Democratic principles—and that together we will march toward a Democratic victory in 1980.

And someday, long after this convention, long after the signs come down, and the crowds stop cheering, and the bands stop playing, may it be said of our campaign that we kept the faith. May it be said of our party in 1980 that we found our faith again.

May it be said of us, both in dark passages and in bright days, in the words of Tennyson that my brothers quoted and loved—and that have special meaning for me now:

I am a part of all that I have met . . .
Tho much is taken, much abides . . .
That which we are, we are—
One equal temper of heroic hearts . . . strong in will
To strive, to seek, to find, and not to yield.

For me, a few hours ago, this campaign came to an end. For all those whose cares have been our concern, the work goes on, the cause endures, the hope still lives, and the dream shall never die.

POLITICAL PLURALISM AND RELIGIOUS ABSOLUTISM[1]

Patricia Roberts Harris[2]

In the 1980 election campaign, a group of fundamentalist preachers launched a drive to bring "old-time religion into the

[1] Public lecture delivered at Princeton University, Princeton, New Jersey, in the Woodrow Wilson Auditorium at 8 p.m. on September 23, 1980.
[2] For biographical note, see Appendix.

voting booth." Led by religious television stars such as the Reverend Jerry Falwell, whose "Old-Time Gospel Hour" is carried by 681 radio and television stations and reaches 18 million or more viewers a week, the movement aimed to enlist from 30 to 65 million evangelical Christians in a political crusade based on fundamentalist morality. Falwell, whose fund-raising operations, according to *Newsweek* (S. 15, '80), yield at least a million dollars a week, headed the Moral Majority, the most active of the fundamentalist political groups. The Moral Majority and the Christian Voice embarked on a voter registration drive among evangelicals, large numbers of whom had not bothered to vote in the past. Through rallies and massive direct mailings, they hoped to create a voting bloc large enough to determine the outcome in several races.

The movement was spurred in part by disillusionment with born-again Christian President Jimmy Carter's position on several issues and by fear of what they believed to be a tide of "secular humanism" sweeping through the government. Leaders were particularly distressed by Carter's support of the Equal Rights Amendment, his failure to halt federally paid abortions, and his defense of the rights of homosexuals. Buoyed by their success in defeating two liberal United States senators and in electing one governor in 1978, they drew up a "hit list" of senators and other elected officials from Washington down to the state and local levels.

One of their most controversial acts was Christian Voice's rating of members of Congress on how they voted on fourteen "key moral issues." What disturbed some observers was that they rated the congressmen not only on "pro-family" issues such as abortion, the Equal Rights Amendment, and gay rights, but that they included such clearly secular issues as the strategic-arms limitations treaty and tax proposals. Others were upset by irresponsible statements such as Falwell's admittedly false account of a totally fabricated meeting he and other evangelicals claimed to have had with President Carter in the White House and assertions by other evangelicals that it was a sin not to vote and that God did not hear the prayers of Jews.

Several prominent clergymen spoke out against the idea that there is "a Christian vote." Among them were the Rev. Billy Graham, Rev. Theodore Hesburg, president of Notre Dame University, the Right Rev. Paul Moore Jr., Episcopal Bishop of New York, Rev. Charles Bergstrom, executive director of the Lutheran

Church, Dr. M. William Howard, president of the National Council of Churches, and Rabbi Marc Tanenbaum of the American Jewish Committee. Lacking the facilities of the Electronic Church to reach a large audience, it is questionable whether the dissent of these leaders had any significant influence on the efforts of the Moral Majority.

Following the election of conservative Ronald Reagan and a Republican majority in the Senate, the defeat of four of the targeted six liberal senators, and other successes, the Moral Majority claimed a large share of credit for the final outcome. Others attributed the vote to disappointment with President Carter's and the Democrat's inability to resolve our domestic and international problems.

On September 23, 1980, long before election day, Patricia Roberts Harris addressed the issue of the wisdom of the judging the performance of elected political representatives on the basis of religious beliefs in a speech to the American Whig-Cliosophic Society at Princeton University. Mrs. Harris at the time was Secretary of the Department of Health and Human Services. She had formerly served as Secretary of Health, Education, and Welfare and as Secretary of Housing and Urban Development. Mrs. Harris is a former Dean of the Law School at Howard University. She is the recipient of thirty-eight honorary degrees and almost as many other awards and citations.

Founded in 1795, the American Whig-Cliosophic Society claims to be the oldest political and debating society in the world. The society is very active and "has the largest student membership of any extra-curricular activity on campus" at Princeton. A large advertisement in the student newspaper the day of the speech stressed that the public was invited. According to *The Daily Princetonian*, Secretary Harris spoke to "a packed audience" in the Woodrow Wilson School Auditorium which seats approximately 250 people. She began her speech at 8 P.M. Her audience was composed of Princeton undergraduates, graduates, and faculty members, and townspeople.

Mrs. Harris stated her theme and concern early in the speech, saying:

> I have no quarrel with the right of individuals and groups—no matter what their political positions—to become involved in the political process. I have sought such involvement all my life. At the same time, however, there are aspects

and implications of these particular efforts which pose a serious threat to the American democratic process and to-night I want to discuss my reasons for believing this to be the case.

My chief concern is that fundamentalist politics at this time is at best exclusionary and at worst a dangerous, intoler-ant, and polarizing influence in our political system.

In recent weeks newspaper columns and the television airwaves have been filled with the allegedly new phenome-non of the entry of American Evangelicals into the elective political process. The news-cum-entertainment program (or is it the other way around) "60 Minutes" this week gave us the unedifying spectacle of overt threats to targeted political figures because they failed to agree with the political position of putative religious leaders on several issues.

That "Sixty Minutes" has reported the phenomenon con-firms its reality and, indeed, its pervasiveness. What we need to remember is that this invasion of the political process by those purporting to act in the name of religion is neither new nor a matter for entertainment.

Two hundred and one years ago, in 1779, Thomas Jeffer-son condemned such activity by religious leaders, saying in the preamble to a bill on religious freedom which he had in-troduced in the Virginia legislature:

Our civil rights have no dependence on our religious opinions, any more than our opinions in physics and geometry; therefore, the proscribing of any citizen as unworthy of the public confi-dence by laying upon him an incapacity of being called to office of public trust . . . unless he profess or renounce this or that religious opinion, is depriving him injuriously of those privileges and ad-vantages to which he has a natural right.

Thomas Jefferson was born into a society acutely aware of the danger of an official relationship between religious and political institutions. Requirements of religious orthodoxy had caused churning of the political life of England from which the early settlers derived so much of their political perception. Every school-boy and girl is taught that the pil-grims came to Plymouth seeking religious freedom. Few understand how little there was for those who refused to accept the orthodoxy of the dominant protestants who led the Massachusetts Bay colony.

Anne Hutchinson's belief that God's love is communicated immediately to the regenerate and that this love serves as a guide to action without mediation of the clergy was considered politically subversive and she was banished from the Massachusetts Bay colony by John Cotton.

Thus our founding fathers had early and significant experience with the demand of religous leaders and their flocks for acceptance of a particular theology, and the insistence that political punishment would result from failure to accept the orthodox religious opinion.

The result was the adoption of George Mason's eloquent provision for religious freedom in the first Virginia Bill of Rights adopted in 1776, which was the forerunner of the first amendment to the constitution of the United States. His provision read:

That religion, or the duty which we owe to our creator, and the manner of discharging it, can be directed only by reason and conviction, not by force or violence; and therefore all men are equally entitled to the free exercise of religion, according the dictates of conscience; and that it is the mutual duty of all to practice christian forebearance, love and charity towards each other.

George Mason would undoubtedly be appalled today—two hundred and four years after Virginia adopted this statement of tolerance—to discover the following:

—An organization called "The Moral Majority"—founded just a little over a year ago by a fundamentalist minister from Virginia—has 400,000 members nationwide and is forming political action committees in all 50 states to distribute $1.5 million to political candidates who it determines favor a "pro-Christian" viewpoint.

—During last spring's "Washington for Jesus" rally, a number of participants visited the office of a southern senator and they informed him that he scored only 23 percent in a "morality rating" prepared by Christian Voice, a political committee organized by right wing Californians. They de-

manded that he fall on his knees and pray for forgiveness.
When he refused, he was targeted for defeat in the fall elections.

—Evangelical leaders and conservative politicians gathered last month in Dallas for two days of oratory and political
activism strategy sessions. At that meeting in Dallas, the New
York *Times* quoted one leader as saying:

> It is interesting at great political rallies how you have a Protes-
> tant to pray, a Catholic to pray, and then you have a Jew to pray.
> With all due respect to those dear people, my friends, God Al-
> mighty does not hear the prayer of the Jew.

He has refused to withdraw the statement.

There is none of the "Christian forebearance, love and
charity towards each other" urged by George Mason in these
three examples.

These three reports do illustrate the nature of the growing
involvement of fundamentalist religious organizations in the
political process. Furthermore, the preponderance of this involvement is on the right, rather than the left, side of the political spectrum.

Now before going any further in my examination of this
phenomenon and its danger to previously accepted political
values, let me make several important points.

First of all, I do not intend to become involved in any discussion of the personal religious beliefs of any individuals or
groups. The freedom to hold religious convictions and to
worship freely is fundamental to both the constitution and
the very soul of this nation. I do not propose to talk about religion per se, but only about the nature of religious participation in the secular, partisan political process.

Second, I do not imply that all "born again" Christians
reflect a right-wing, or even conservative, political outlook.
Any number of evangelical Christians—President Carter,
Senator Mark Hatfield and former Senator Harold Hughes,
for example, hold decidedly different views. The vast majority of such individuals believe in and practice toleration of
opposing views and vote as most of us vote—on the basis of

deeply felt beliefs about priorities and goals, parties and candidates—and their votes are therefore widely distributed all across the political spectrum.

Nor do I imply that all evangelical Christians want their churches or other religious organizations to participate in a direct and particular way in political campaigns.

There is evidence, however, that significant numbers of evangelical Christian organizations are moving toward intense involvement in elective politics and that they have become a major factor in energizing right-wing politics in our country.

The terms "born again" and "evangelical" have been popularly applied to individuals who attest to having had a personal religious experience which has changed their lives. A large number of these individuals, in addition to experiencing a personal conversion, also hold to a stricter or more "fundamental" interpretation of the scripture.

The American religious tradition is a rich and varied one, and the distinction between the evangelical and more "establishment" religious experience is as old as the country. What is significant about the trend today is that the number of "born again" Christians seems to be steadily on the rise. Public opinion polls have tried to measure the number of Americans in that category, and although they do not agree on a number, they variously estimate it to be between 35 and 60 million.

In the last few years we have seen evidence of the trend in large rallies like the one held in Washington last May. We have also seen rapid growth in the so-called "Christian oriented" media—several hundred television and radio outlets which are now devoted primarily to religious programming.

The growing activism of such religious groups can also be seen in the political arena. At the session of fundamentalist leaders in Dallas last month, one evangelist said, "not voting is a sin against Almighty God," and he urged his audience to "crawl out from under those padded pews." According to one newspaper account, "attentions swung widely from theology and scripture to instruction on how to organize without violating tax laws, the practicality of registering a congregation to vote during the Sunday service and the importance of keeping a 'moral score card' on the voting records of elected representatives."

I have no quarrel with the right of individuals and groups—no matter what their political positions—to become involved in the political process. I have sought such involvement all my life. At the same time, however, there are aspects and implications of these particular efforts which pose a serious threat to the American democratic process and tonight I want to discuss my reasons for believing this to be the case.

My chief concern is that fundamentalist politics as practiced at this time is at best exclusionary and at worst a dangerous, intolerant, and polarizing influence in our political system.

At the recent Dallas conference speaker after speaker denounced "perverts, radicals, leftists, communists, liberals and humanists" who presumably have taken over the country and are actively seeking its destruction. This kind of overt "us against them" appeal—the "God-fearing" against the "heathen"—has roots in virtually every generation in American history. At various times it has made victims of Catholics, immigrants, Jews, blacks, Indians and countless others who failed to fit into neat patterns of acceptability. In my judgment, at least, there are undercurrents of many of the same prejudices in much of the new right rhetoric today.

One slightly more subtle example of exclusionary practices is the so-called "Christian yellow pages"—a telephone directory, similar to the one in popular use, that lists only "born again" merchants and exhorts Christians to restrict their business to those establishments.

George Will—a columnist, a graduate of Princeton, and a man few regard as a radical, a leftist, or even a humanist—described such an appeal as "an act of aggression against a pluralistic society." He added "discrimination condoned—indeed, incited—in commerce will not be confined to commerce."

Although the majority of the people of the country classify themselves as Christian, the nation has consistently, painfully, and with great success moved from intolerance to toleration of both political and religious dissent.

We Americans have, in this century, truly come to agree with Voltaire that we may "disagree with what you say, but we will fight to the death for your right to say it" because we recognize the value of both political dissenters and of non-Christian traditions. Our democracy has functioned because, as a rule, we have sought out common ground—shared values and beliefs, rather than an orthodoxy espoused by any particular group. The end result may not have pleased everyone, but it has offered to each individual a reasonable measure of freedom in which to exercise his or her civil and human rights.

That consensus orientation is profoundly threatened by those who advocate a "Christian crusade" or who want our leadership narrowed to include only "pro Christian" public officials.

In this particular campaign, fundamentalist organizations seek to identify "pro-Christian" candidates with a measuring stick of very specific issues. More often than not, the connection between Christian scripture and such concerns is mystifying.

I am sure that I need not remind this audience of the positions fundamentalist groups have taken on our most pressing and most controversial social issues.

In a time of rapid and often disconcerting change in social and moral values, right wing political operatives are working hard to cultivate votes among the distressed. Direct scriptural guidance is cited in determining the "Christian position" on such issues as equal rights for women, gun control, abortion, sex education in schools, and pornography. I grant the existence of profound moral issues in the debate on the legality of funding of abortion, but I can find only a political basis for being opposed to gun control.

Earlier, I mentioned a senator's meeting with a group who rated him "poor" on a moral score card. His so-called "morality rating" took into account his positions on such issues as recognition of Taiwan as the legitimate Chinese government, prayer in the public schools, a balanced budget, sanctions against the former Rhodesian government, and creation of the Federal Department of Education.

A 1978 candidate for Congress in Virginia, himself an evangelical minister, saw a direct biblical admonition against welfare programs, called the income tax "unscriptural" and declared that "the free market is the biblical approach to economics."

A senator who was defeated in 1978, largely because of his vote in support of the Panama Canal treaties, said an astonishing number of letters from his constituents admonished him "as a Christian" to vote against ratification.

In sheer exasperation, another former senator, Harold Hughes—a Christian evangelist himself—said recently, "I have searched the scriptures diligently and I have not found one word in them on Jesus Christ's position on the Panama Canal. To say you've got to believe this or that in the political arena or you are not a Christian is absolute blasphemy."

Whether you agree or disagree with the position fundamentalist organizations have taken on these issues is beside the point. What is important are the underlying premises which serve as the basis for their views: that this is a "Christian" and not a pluralistic society; that the nation must achieve its "Christian" destiny by adhering to a specific set of positions derived from scripture as interpreted by a particular theological school and that the imposition of those beliefs on the nation as a whole is not only permissible, but desirable.

The consequences of the demand for orthodoxy enforced by the political process are found throughout history, from Socrates to the victims of the Ayatollah Khomeini. For those who assert that their restrictive interpretations are essential to the well-being of this country, I would remind them that the theory that the world was round was denied by certain theologians as little as fifty years before "Columbus sailed the ocean blue." If we could speak to Galileo about whether the "Christian" position on Copernican theory and his own work on astronomy was in the best interest of that genius or the world he served, he might well suggest that if the fundamentalism of his time had prevailed, its modern U.S. proponents would live in Europe, and Indians would still own this land. The association of church and state, the identity of interest of Aristotelian professors who disagreed with Galileo's ideas, and their ability to end his freedom and halt his work are some of the inevitable consequences of the achievement of the kind of identity of theology and public policy that our political evangelicals appear to seek today.

We have conveniently forgotten that Scopes was convicted of violating the law when he taught the theory of evolution, which some fundamentalists still oppose. That conviction was in this century.

On one issue which the radical right refuses to leave alone—prayer in the school—the lack of respect for difference, and the insistence upon using government to achieve particular Christian theological ends is most blatant and most intolerant. That Jews, Moslems, Buddhists or non-believers must have the time and nature of their relationship with the deity determined by the state runs counter to George Mason's Virginia Bill of Rights and to the Bill of Rights of the Constitution. Such a position is blatantly intolerant of both of the religious and non-believers and takes us back to days of religious inquisitions that I thought we had rejected in this country with the adoption of our Bill of Rights.

The damage such viewpoints do by excluding large number of people from full participation in the nation's present and future is difficult to assess, but the problem of exclusion is exacerbated by the righteous fervor with which these political fundamentalists approach the debate.

This is especially painful for other Christians who do not share a right wing viewpoint.

Public officials today regularly encounter citizens who tell them how "real Christians" would vote or act—or how "real Christians" will repay an errant representative for his sins. This offends me because I care about what my Jewish and Buddhist and Bahai brothers and sisters believe about an issue and I want to be sure that what I do is as broadly acceptable to their ethical system as I can make it.

Republican senator Mark Hatfield wrote: "During my opposition to the Vietnam war, the religious segment of the radical right attacked not only my patriotism, but the authenticity of my personal Christian faith."

When the argument is so presented, there is no room for discussion of the issues. Politics—that crucible of ambiguities and compromises, choices and alternatives—degenerates into a raw power struggle in which one side impugns the other's religious sincerity and the judgment of how to act is based on numbers of votes, and not the validity of the idea. To argue that there is a single "Christian" viewpoint or even a religious point of view on every issue in foreign and domestic policy is to say no debate is necessary or desirable—that all that is required is unquestioning obedience of "God's will" as revealed to a single individual or group. I thought that was what the last four hundred years had rejected.

That kind of moral absolutism is alien to the best of the American experience, and it is sobering to note that one country in which such a totalitarian interpretation of "God's will" is today practiced is Iran. In that nation the rich variety of Islamic culture has been trampled by religious zealots who profess to know the one truth and who are willing to impose their narrow interpretation of Moslem principles on the entire nation.

Our own country has been nurtured and sustained in a more tolerant atmosphere. Even in the darkest days of the Civil War, Abraham Lincoln reminded the country that both North and South pray to the same God, and when he invoked the deity, he understood that we see the right only "as God gives us to see the right."

That spirit of humility and tolerance which so characterized Lincoln is much needed today. The absolute certainty with which some individuals approach the political battle— and the arrogance with which they propose a crusade to "re-Christianize" America—is dangerous for our democracy. I am beginning to fear that we could have an Ayatollah Khomeini in this country, but that he will not have a beard, but he will have a television program.

I would argue that the politicization of evangelical Christianity is bad for religion. As Paul Tillich reminded us, "Doubt is not the opposite of faith; it is an element of faith." Those who measure their piety and the piety of others with "moral score cards" are the modern day pharisees, and they do themselves, as well as their nation, no service. We may find that equating religious position with particular political positions will lead to rejection of both. The founding fathers of this nation were religious men, and they did not seek to divorce religious, moral, and ethical beliefs from the practice of politics. They knew that such beliefs are the foundation on which political philosophies are based. But at the same time, they pointedly chose to separate church and state because they did not want one particular group, or one particular point of view, to dominate all the others. They knew the result of failure to separate church and state could be excommunication from the polity as well as excommunication from the church, as happened to both Galileo and Anne Hutchinson.

Our society—infinitely more pluralistic today than was the America of 1789—needs to re-examine that premise and reaffirm our commitment to that principle.

Pluralism requires political discipline on the part of the majority. Any majority has the power in a democracy to eliminate the minority or to eliminate the expression of the ideas of the minority. It is the essence of democracy that the majority protects, respects and listens to its minorities.

Neither political nor religious absolutism is consistent with the United States democratic assumption that unfettered debate may lead to a change of mind on issue.

It is ironic that the political absolutism with which we are faced today finds its center of support in Protestant groups. That very name is a reminder that these denominations grew out of a protest against religious absolutism.

Reinhold Niebuhr reminded us that "we must never confuse our fragmentary apprehension of the truth with the truth itself." Our political system rests on our having the humility to remember that fact, and act accordingly.

None of us knows a single truth which closes the debate

and dictates our actions in the political world, but in a democracy we can work together in the search for truth and in doing so create the just and humane society which all of us seek.

Although the first amendment directs itself to the Congress in its prohibition of the establishment of religion, the history out of which it came, and the intent with which it was adopted were clearly part of the movement of this country to a toleration of differences and encouragement of dissent. That these two concerns must live side by side with the right of the majority to make decisions if no consensus can be reached, and no compromise adopted, does not say that the majority has the right to refuse to seek consensus and compromise.

There is hope that for all the attention garnered by the religious absolutists in this campaign, the people of this nation have understood and accepted the admonition of religious freedom of George Mason and Thomas Jefferson. In Boston last week, voters backed candidates denounced from the pulpit of their church.

The Des Moines, Iowa *Register* reported on September 14 that a new Iowa poll showed the Iowans overwhelmingly disapprove of religious leaders urging their followers to vote for specific candidates, and only four percent of those polled said they would be persuaded to vote for a candidate if their religious leader asked them to do so.

Before we become too optimistic about these results, it should be pointed out that four percent would be enough to determine a close election.

The solution, of course, is for the majority that supports rationality and consensus to go to the polls, vote their informed consensus, and, in so doing, again overwhelm the forces of bigotry and polarization.

If they stay home, absolutism will win and we may be required to begin again the battle for humanism, rationality, and the democratic spirit which we thought had been won with the Declaration of Independence and the Bill of Rights of the United States Constitution.

THE STATE OF THE JUDICIARY

ADDRESS TO THE AMERICAN BAR ASSOCIATION[1]

WARREN E. BURGER[2]

Since becoming Chief Justice of the United States Supreme Court, Warren E. Burger has delivered an annual "state of the judiciary" address to the American Bar Association. On February 8, 1981, he presented his twelfth report to the association at its mid-year meeting in Houston, Texas. The convention, which began on February 2 and was to continue until February 11, included business and educational programs and speeches by prominent legal and political spokesmen. The Chief Justice delivered his 35-minute speech at mid-afternoon in the "regal-red" Imperial Ballroom of the Hyatt Regency Hotel to an audience of approximately 2,000 American Bar Association officers, House of Delegates, Board of Governors, members, staff, and representatives of the media.

In the speech, Justice Burger enunciated several controversial proposals, notably curtailing bail and the right of appeal and he called for massive expenditures to combat crime, which attracted national attention and provoked sharp disagreement. The Washington *Post* characterized Burger's speech as "the most startling of his long career." Linda Greenhouse, writing for the New York *Times* observed that the "speech was a significant departure for the Chief Justice and there was little doubt that it was a calculated one. The image he drew of an 'impotent America,' undergoing 'a reign of terror' and held hostage to crime was startling rhetoric for any national figure to use, let alone a Chief Justice." (F. 10, '81). The Washington *Post* described the speech as "the most startling of his long career" and his "broadest and most vehement on the subject of crime." (F. 9, '81). The Chicago *Tribune* labeled it "an uncommonly bold speech . . . with an explicitness that he has in the past avoided." (F. 10, '81). The *Christian Science Monitor* concluded, "If United States Chief Justice Warren Burger aimed to

[1] Delivered to the annual convention of the American Bar Association in the Imperial Ballroom of the Hyatt Regency Hotel, Houston, Texas, in mid-afternoon on February 8, 1981.
[2] For biographical note, see Appendix.

shock those involved in civil liberties and criminal justice with his speech, . . . he has succeeded." (F. 10, '81)

The response to the speech was mostly favorable, with the audience of lawyers interrupting him with applause eight times. Leon Jaworski, former Watergate prosecutor and former ABA president, praised the speech as "bold, very courageous, and somewhat innovative." Favorable newspaper editorial reactions described the speech as "much-needed," "accurate," "laudable," and "significant."

Not all who heard or read the speech responded positively. The Chicago *Tribune* noted that "the speech sent shivers up and down the spines of many civil libertarians and minority group leaders." (F. 23, '81). The Philadelphia *Inquirer* claimed "his position could be taken as the equivalent of shouting fire in a crowded theater packed with the constitutional guarantees which almost two centuries of U.S. justice have developed and preserved." (F. 10, '81) Bruce Ennis, national legal director of the American Civil Liberties Union called it a "simplistic, short-term solution to crime in America." It was also called "dangerous" and criticized as raising serious constitutional questions.

Burger, whose speeches in the past have often charted new directions, worked on the speech for seven months and was believed to consider it the start of a major push for changes beyond what he could do in Supreme Court opinions. Although the speech surprised—and stunned—many, several journalists pointed out that as early as 1967 while still a federal appeals court judge Burger had taken a similar position. Indeed that 1967 speech was cited by Richard M. Nixon as one of the factors that prompted him to select Burger as chief justice.

Today, for the twelfth time, you allow me this opportunity to lay before you problems concerning the administration of justice, as I see them from my chair. For this, Mr. President and Fellow Members of the Association, I thank you.

On previous occasions I have discussed with you a range of needs of our system. Your responses beginning in 1969 were a major factor in bringing into being the Institute for Court Management, The National Center for State Courts, The Provision for Court Administrators in the Federal System, and many other changes. And in light of my subject today, I should also mention the important contributions made beginning in 1970 by your Commission on Correctional Facilities and Services. The value of these improvements is beyond precise calculation. But the value is great. We do not always agree, but our differences are few indeed. All I ask for is equal time.

The new President who has just taken office is confronted with a host of great problems, domestic and worldwide: inflation, unemployment, energy, an overblown government, a breakdown of our educational system, a weakening of family ties, and a vast increase in crime. As he looks beyond our shores, he sees grave, long-range problems, which begin ninety miles off the shores of Florida and extend around the globe.

Today I will focus on a single subject, although one of large content. Crime and the fear of crime have permeated the fabric of American life, damaging the poor and minorities even more than the affluent. A recent survey indicates forty-six percent of women and forty-eight percent of Negroes are "significantly frightened" by pervasive crime in America.

Seventy-five years ago, Roscoe Pound shook this association with his speech on "The Causes of Popular Dissatisfaction with the Administration of Justice." In the 1976 Pound Conference, we reviewed his great critique but also examined criminal justice. My distinguished colleague, Judge Leon Higginbotham, carefully noted the imperative need for balance, in criminal justice, between the legitimate rights of the accused and the right of all others, including the victims. And, of course, we are all victims of every crime.

When I speak of "Crime and Punishment" I embrace the entire spectrum beginning with an individual's first contact with police authority through the stages of arrest, investigation, adjudication and corrective confinement. At every stage the system cries out for change, and I do not exclude the adjudicatory stage. At each step in this process the primary goal, for both the individual and society, is protection and security. This theme runs throughout all history.

When our distant ancestors came out of caves and rude tree dwellings thousands of years ago to form bands and tribes and later towns, villages and cities, they did so to satisfy certain fundamental human needs: Mutual protection, human companionship, and later for trade and commerce. But the basic need was *security*—security of the person, the family, the home and of property. Taken together, this is the meaning of a civilized society.

Today, the proud American boast that we are the most civilized, most prosperous, most peace-loving people leaves a bitter aftertaste. We have prospered. We are, and have been, peace-loving in our relations with other nations. But, like it or not, today here at home we are approaching the status of an impotent society—a society whose capability of maintaining elementary security on the streets, in schools, and for the homes of our people is in doubt.

I thought of this recently in a visit to the medieval city of Bologna, Italy. There, still standing are walled enclaves of a thousand years ago with a high corner tower where watch was kept for roving hostile street gangs. When the householder left his barricaded enclave he had a company of spearmen and others with cross-bows and battle-axes as guards.

Possibly some of our problem of behavior stems from the fact that we have virtually eliminated from public schools and higher education any effort to teach values of integrity, truth, personal accountability and respect for others' rights. This was recently commented on by a distinguished world statesman, Dr. Charles Malik, former president of the U.N. General Assembly. Speaking to a conference on education, he said:

I search in vain for any reference to the fact that character, personal integrity, spiritual depth, the highest moral standards, the wonderful living values of the great tradition, have anything to do with the business of the university or with the world of learning.

Perhaps what Dr. Malik said is not irrelevant to what gives most Americans such deep concern in terms of behavior in America today.

I pondered long before deciding to concentrate today on this sensitive subject of crime, and I begin by reminding ourselves that under our enlightened Constitution and Bill of Rights, whose bicentennials we will soon celebrate, we have established a system of criminal justice that provides more protection, more safeguards, more guarantees for those accused of crime than any other nation in all history. The protective armor we give to each individual when the State brings a charge is great indeed. This protection was instituted—and it has expanded steadily since the turn of this century—because of our profound fear of the power of Kings and States developed by an elite class to protect the status quo—their status above all else—and it was done at the expense of the great masses of ordinary people.

Two hundred years ago we changed that. Indeed, in the past 30 or 40 years we have changed it so much that some now question whether the changes have produced a dangerous imbalance.

I put to you this question: Is a society redeemed if it provides massive safeguards for accused persons including pretrial freedom for most crimes, defense lawyers at public expense, trials, and appeals, re-trials and more appeals—almost without end—and yet fails to provide elementary protection for its law-abiding citizens? I ask you to ponder this question as you hear me out.

Time does not allow—nor does my case require—that I burden you with masses of detailed statistics—I assure you the statistics are not merely grim, they are frightening. Let me begin near home: Washington, D.C., the capital of our enlightened country, in 1980 had more criminal homicides than Sweden and Denmark combined with an aggregate population of over twelve million as against 650,000 for Washington, D.C. and Washington is not unique. From New York City, to Los Angeles, to Miami the story on increase in violent crime from 1979 to 1980 is much the same. New York City with about the same population as Sweden has 20 times as many homicides. The United States has one hundred times the rate of burglary of Japan. Overall violent crime in the United

States increased sharply from 1979 to 1980, continuing a double-digit rate. More than one-quarter of all the households in this country are victimized by some kind of criminal activity at least once each year.

The New York *Times* recently reported that one documented study estimated that the chances of any person arrested for a felony in New York City of being punished in any way—apart from the arrest record—were 108 to 1! And it is clear that thousands of felonies go unreported in that city as in all others.

For at least ten years many of our national leaders and those of other countries, have spoken of international terrorism, but our rate of routine, day-by-day terrorism in almost any large city exceeds the casualties of all the reported "international terrorists" in any given year.

Why do we show such indignation over alien terrorists and such tolerance for the domestic variety?

Must we be hostages within the borders of our own self-styled enlightened, civilized country? Accurate figures on the cost of home burglar alarms, of three locks on each door—and sadly, of handgun sales for householders—are not available but they run into hundreds of millions of dollars.

What the American people want is that crime and criminals be brought under control so that we can be safe on the streets and in our homes and for our children to be safe in schools and at play. Today that safety is fragile.

It needs no more recital of the frigtening facts and statistics to focus attention on the problem—a problem easier to define than to correct. We talk of having criminals make restitution or have the state compensate the victims. The first is largely unrealistic, the second is unlikely. Neither meets the central problem. Nothing will bring about swift changes in the terror that stalks our streets and endangers our homes, but I will make a few suggestions.

To do this I must go back over some history which may help explain our dilemma.

For a quarter of a century I regularly spent my vacations visiting courts and prisons in other countries, chiefly Western Europe. My mentors in this educational process were two of the outstanding penologists of our time: the late James V. Bennett, Director of the United States Bureau of Prisons and the late Torsten Ericksson, his counterpart in Sweden, where crime rates were once low, poverty was nonexistent, correctional systems enlightened and humane. Each was a vigorous advocate of using prisons for educational and vocational training.

I shared and still share with them the belief that poverty and unemployment are reflected in crime rates—chiefly crimes against property. But if poverty were the principal cause of crime as was the easy explanation given for so many years, crime would have been almost nonexistent in affluent Sweden and very high in Spain and Portugal. But the hard facts simply did not and do not support the easy claims that poverty is the controlling factor; it is just one factor. America's crime rate today exceeds our crime rate during the great depression.

We must not be misled by cliches and slogans that if we but abolish proverty crime will also disappear. There is more to it than that. A far greater factor is the deterrent effect of swift and certain consequences: swift arrest, prompt trial, certain penalty, and—at some point—finality of judgment.

To speak of crime in America and not mention the drugs and drug-related crime would be an oversight of large dimension. The destruction of lives by drugs is more frightening than all the homicides we suffer. The victims are not just the young who become addicts. Their families and, in turn, their victims and all of society suffer over a lifetime. I am not wise enough to venture a solution. Until we effectively seal our many thousands of miles of borders—which would require five or ten times the present border guard personnel and vastly enlarge the internal drug enforcement staffs, there is little else we can do. Our Fourth and Fifth Amendments and statutes give the same broad protection to drug pushers as they give to you and me, the judges are oath-bound to apply those commands.

It is clear that there is a startling amount of crime committed by persons on release awaiting trial, on parole, and on probation release. It is not uncommon for an accused to finally be brought to trial with two, three or more charges pending. Overburdened prosecutors and courts tend to drop other pending charges when one conviction is obtained. Should we be surprised if the word gets around in the "criminal community" that you can commit two or three crimes for the price of only one and that there is not much risk in committing crimes while awaiting trial?

Deterrence is the primary core of any effective response to the reign of terror in American cities. Deterrence means speedy action by society, but that process runs up against the reality that many large cities have either reduced their police forces or failed to keep them in balance with double-digit crime inflation.

A first step to achieve deterrence is to have larger forces of better trained officers. Thanks to the F.B.I. Academy we have the pattern for such training.

A second step is to re-examine statutes on pre-trial release at every level. This requires that there be a sufficient number of investigators, prosecutors, and defenders—and judges—to bring defendants to trial swiftly. Any study of the statistics will reveal that "bail crime" reflects a great hole in the fabric of our protection against internal terrorism.

To change this melancholy picture will call for spending more money than we have ever before devoted to law enforcement, and even this will be for naught if we do not reexamine our judicial process and philosophy with respect to finality of judgments. The search for "perfect" justice has led us on a course found nowhere else in the world. A true miscarriage of justice, whether 20-, 30- or 40-years old, should always be open to review, but the judicial process becomes a mockery of justice if it is forever open to appeals and retrials for errors in the arrest, the search, or the trial. Traditional appellate review is the cure for errors, but we have forgotten that simple truth.

Our search for true justice must not be twisted into an endless quest for technical errors unrelated to guilt or innocence.

The system has gone so far that Judge Henry Friendly, in

proposing to curb abuses of collateral attack, entitled his article, "Is Innocence Irrelevant?"

And Justice Jackson once reminded us that the Constitution should not be read as a "suicide pact."

Each of these men, of course, echoed what another great jurist, Justice Benjamin Cardozo, wrote more than fifty years ago in his essays on "the nature of the judicial process."

I am not advocating a new idea but merely restating an old one that we have ignored. At this point, judicial discretion and judicial restraint require me to stop and simply to repeat that governments were instituted and exist chiefly to protect people. If governments fail in this basic duty they are not excused, they are not redeemed by showing that they have established the most perfect systems to protect the claims of defendants in criminal cases. A government that fails to protect both the rights of accused persons and also all other people has failed in its mission. I leave it to you whether the balance has been fairly struck.

Let me now try to place this in perspective: first, the bail reform statutes of recent years, especially as to non-violent crimes, were desirable and overdue; second, the provisions for a lawyer for every defendant were desirable and overdue; third, statutes to insure speedy trials are desirable but only if the same legislation provides the means to accomplish the objective.

Many enlightened countries succeed in holding criminal trials within four to eight weeks after arrest. First non-violent offenders are generally placed on probation, free to return to a gainful occupation under close supervision. But I hardly need remind this audience that our criminal process often goes on two, three, four or more years before the accused runs out all the options. Even after sentence and confinement, the warfare continues with endless streams of petitions for writs, suits against parole boards, wardens and judges.

So we see a paradox—even while we struggle toward correction, education and rehabilitation of the offender, our system encourages prisoners to continue warfare with society. The result is that whatever may have been the defendant's hostility toward the police, the witnesses, the prosecutors, the judge and jurors—and the public defender who failed to win his case—those hostilities are kept alive. How much chance do you think there is of changing or rehabilitating a person who is encouraged to keep up years of constant warfare with society?

The dismal failure of our system to stem the flood of crime repeaters is reflected in part in the massive number of those who go in and out of prisons. In a nation that has been thought to be the world leader in so many areas of human activity our system of justice—not simply the prisons—produces the world's highest rate of "recall" for those who are processed through it. How long can we tolerate this rate of recall and the devastation it produces?

What I suggest now—and this association with its hundreds of state and local affiliates can be a powerful force—is a "damage control program." It will be long; it will be controversial; it will be costly—but less costly than the billions in dollars and thousands of blighted lives now hostage to crime.

To do this is as much a part of our national defense as the Pentagon budget.

Sometimes we speak glibly of a "war on crime." A war is indeed being waged but it is a war by a small segment of society against the whole of society. Now a word of caution: That "war" will not be won simply by harsher sentences; not by harsh mandatory minimum sentence statutes; not by abandoning the historic guarantees of the Bill of Rights. And perhaps, above all, it will not be accomplished by self-appointed armed citizen police patrols. At age 200, this country has outgrown the idea of private law and vigilantes. Volunteer community watchman services are quite another matter.

Now let me present the ultimate paradox: After society has spent years and often a modest fortune to put just one person behind bars, we become bored. The media lose interest and the individual is forgotten. Our humanitarian concern evaporates. In all but a minority of the states we confine the person in an overcrowded, understaffed institution with little or no library facilities, little if any educational program or vocational training. I have visited American prisons built more than 100 years ago for 800 prisoners, but with two thousand crowded today inside their ancient walls.

Should you look at the records you will find that the 300,-000 persons now confined in penal institutions are heavily weighted with offenders under age thirty. A majority of them cannot meet minimum standards of reading, writing, and arithmetic. Plainly this goes back to our school systems. A sample of this was reflected in a study of pupils in a large city where almost half of the third graders failed reading. This should not surprise us, for today we find some high school graduates who cannot read or write well enough to hold simple jobs.

Now turn with me to a few steps which ought to be considered:

(1) Restore to all pretrial release laws the crucial element of dangerousness to the community based on a combination of the evidence then available and the defendant's past record, to deter crime-while-on-bail;

(2) Provide for trial within weeks of arrest for most cases, except for extraordinary cause shown;

(3) Priority for review on appeal within eight weeks of a judgment of guilt;

(4) Following exhaustion of appellate review, confine all subsequent judicial review to claims of miscarriage of justice;

and finally:

A. We must accept the reality that to confine offenders behind walls without trying to change them is an expensive folly with short term benefits—a "winning of battles while losing the war";

B. Provide for generous use of probation for first nonviolent offenders, with intensive supervision and counseling and swift revocation if probation terms are violated;

C. A broad scale program of physical rehabilitation of

the penal institutions to provide a decent setting for expanded educational and vocational training;

D. Make all vocational and educational programs mandatory with credit against the sentence for educational progress—literally a program to "learn the way out of prison," so that no prisoner leaves without at least being able to read, write, do basic arithmetic and have a marketable skill;

E. Generous family visitation in decent surroundings to maintain family ties, with rigid security to exclude drugs or weapons;

F. Counseling services after release paralleling the "after-care" services in Sweden, Holland, Denmark, and Finland. All this should be aimed at developing the prisoner's respect for self, respect for others, accountability for conduct and appreciation of the value of work, of thrift, and of family.

G. Encourage religious groups to give counsel on ethical behavior and occupational adjustment during and after confinement.

The two men I spoke of as my mentors beginning twenty-five years ago—James V. Bennett and Torsten Eriksson of Sweden, were sadly disappointed at the end of their careers, on their great hopes for rehabilitation of offenders. A good many responsible qualified observers are reaching the stage that we must now accept the harsh truth that there may be some incorrigible human beings who cannot be changed except by God's own mercy to that one person. But we cannot yet be certain and in our own interest—in the interest of billions in dollars lost to crime and blighted if not destroyed lives—we must try to deter and try to cure.

This will be costly in the short run and the short run will not be brief. This illness our society suffers has been generations in developing, but we should begin at once to divert the next generation from the dismal paths of the past, to inculcate a sense of personal accountability in each schoolchild to the end that our homes, schools and streets will be safe for all.

JUDICIAL VERBICIDE: AN AFFRONT TO THE CONSTITUTION[1]

Sam J. Ervin Jr.[2]

On October 22, 1980, Sam J. Ervin Jr., former United States Senator from North Carolina, delivered a speech as part of the Hubert H. Humphrey Lectureship in Public Affairs at Louisiana State University. Ervin, a Harvard Law School graduate who likes to say he is "just a country lawyer," is considered a Constitutional expert. He is probably most widely known as chairman of a Senate committee which investigated Watergate in the early 1970s.

Ervin said he came to Baton Rouge to talk about the Constitution and how it is falling victim to false interpretations by the judiciary. "The people of our land are being ruled by the transitory personal notions of justices who occupy, for a fleeting moment of history, seats on the Supreme Court bench, rather than by the enduring precepts of the Constitution," he said. "Judges who perpetrate verbicide are judicial activists, but contrary to popular opinion all judicial activists are not liberals. Some of them are conservatives."

The speech was delivered to an audience of 300–350 students, professors, and interested members of the community in the auditorium of the Hebert Law Center.

Anthony Ward, of the Washington *Post*, claims that Ervin is at his best when arguing the intent and scope of the Constitution, which the Senator calls "the finest thing to come out of the mind of man." Ward notes, "He has not always won the hearts of liberals in doing so" pointing out that:

> . . . during the Civil Rights battles of the early 1960s, he was—in the name of states' rights—a leader in the fight by Southern conservatives to stall, delay, limit, and weaken the major antidiscrimination proposals of those years. But by the late 1960s he had come to be seen as one of the Senate's staunch-

[1] Delivered as part of the Hubert H. Humphrey Lectureship in Public Affairs at the Hebert Law Center, Louisiana State University, Baton Rouge, on October 22, 1980.
[2] For biographical note, see Appendix.

est, and most eloquent, advocates of individual liberties, and one of its strongest opponents of unchecked government power.

Commenting on the speech, the New York *Times* observed that although the former senator was 84 years old and had been suffering from illness he demonstrated that he could still "deliver a hard-hitting speech." (O. 24, '80, B6)

Jim's administrator was suing the railroad for his wrongful death. The first witness he called to the stand testified as follows: "I saw Jim walking up the track. A fast train passed, going up the track. After it passed, I didn't see Jim. I walked up the track a little way and discovered Jim's severed head lying on one side of the track, and the rest of his body on the other." The witness was asked how he reacted to his gruesome discovery. He responded: "I said to myself something serious must have happened to Jim."

Something serious has been happening to constitutional government in America. I want to talk to you about it.

My motive for doing so is as lofty as that which caused Job Hicks to be indicted and convicted of disturbing religious worship in the Superior Court of Burke County, North Carolina, my home county, 75 years ago.

Job revered the word of the Lord. An acquaintance of his, John Watts, took a notion he had been called to preach the gospel and adopted the practice of doing so in any little country church which would allow him to occupy its pulpit. While he was well-versed in his profession as a brick mason, John Watts was woefully ignorant in matters of theology.

One Sunday, Job Hicks imbibed a little too much Burke County corn liquor, a rather potent beverage. After so doing, he walked by a little country church, saw John Watts in the pulpit, and heard him expounding to the congregation his peculiar version of a Biblical text. Job Hicks entered the church, staggered to the pulpit, grabbed John Watts' coat collar, dragged him to the door, and threw him out of the church.

When the time came for the pronouncement of the sentence upon the jury's verdict of guilty, Judge Robinson, the presiding judge, observed: "Mr. Hicks, when you were guilty of such unseemly conduct on the Sabbath Day, you must have been too drunk to realize what you were doing." Job Hicks responded: "It is true, Your Honor, that I had had several drinks, but I wouldn't want Your Honor to think I was so drunk that I could stand by and hear the Word of the Lord being *mummicked up* like that without doing something about it."

Although I am completely sober, I am constrained to confess I am like Job Hicks in one respect. I cannot remain silent while the words of the Constitution are being *mummicked up* by Supreme Court justices.

This is so because I entertain the abiding conviction that the Constitution is our most precious heritage as Americans. When it is interpreted and applied aright, the Constitution protects all human beings within our borders from tyranny on the one hand and anarchy on the other. William Ewart Gladstone, the wise English statesman, correctly described it as the most wonderful work ever struck off at a given time by the brain and purpose of man.

I entitle my remarks "Judicial Verbicide: an Affront To the Constitution." I am prompted to do so by this trenchant truth which was told by Dr. Oliver Wendell Holmes in his *Autocrat of the Breakfast Table:*

> Life and language are alike sacred. Homicide and verbicide— that is—violent treatment of a word with fatal results to its legitimate meaning, which is its life—are alike forbidden.

The term "Founding Fathers" is well-designed to describe those who framed and ratified the Constitution and its first ten amendments. For ease of expression, I also apply it to those who framed and ratified subsequent amendments.

The Founding Fathers knew the history of the struggle of the people against arbitrary governmental power during countless ages for the right to self-rule and freedom from tyranny, and understood the lessons taught by that history.

As a consequence they knew these eternal truths: First, that "whatever government is not a government of laws is a despotism, let it be called what it may"; second, that occupants of public offices love power and are prone to abuse it; and, third, that what autocratic rulers of the people had done in the past might be attempted by their new rulers in the future unless they were restrained by laws which they alone could neither alter nor nullify.

The Founding Fathers desired above all things to secure to the people in a written Constitution every right which they had wrested from autocratic rulers while they were struggling for the right to self-rule and freedom from tyranny.

Their knowledge of history gave them the wisdom to know that this objective could be accomplished only in a government of laws, i.e., a government which rules by certain, constant, and uniform laws rather than by the arbitrary, uncertain, and inconstant wills of impatient men who happen to occupy for a fleeting moment of time legislative, executive, or judicial offices.

For these reasons, the Founding Fathers framed and ratified the Constitution, which they intended to last for the ages, to constitute a law for both rulers and people in war and in peace, and to cover with the shield of its protection all classes of men with impartiality at all times and under all circumstances.

While they intended it to endure for the ages as the nation's basic instrument of government, the Founding Fathers realized that useful alterations of some of its provisions would be suggested by experience.

Consequently, they made provision for its amendment in one way and one way only, i.e., by combined action of Congress and the states as set forth in Article V. By so doing, they ordained that "nothing new can be put into the Constitution except through the amendatory process" and "nothing old can be taken out without the same process"; and thereby forbade Supreme Court justices to attempt to·revise the Constitution while professing to interpret it.

In framing and ratifying the Constitution, the Founding Fathers recognized and applied an everlasting truth embodied by the British philosopher, Thomas Watts, in this phrase:

"Freedom is political power divided into small fragments."

They divided all governmental powers between the federal government and the states by delegating to the former the powers essential to enable it to operate as a national government for all the states, and by reserving to the states all other powers.

They divided among the Congress, the President, and the federal judiciary the powers delegated to the federal government by giving Congress the power to make federal laws, imposing on the President the duty to enforce federal laws, and assigning to the federal judiciary the power to interpret federal laws for all purposes and state laws for the limited purpose of determining their constitutional validity.

In making this division of powers, the Founding Fathers vested in the Supreme Court as the head of the federal judiciary the awesome authority to determine with finality whether governmental action, federal or state, harmonizes with the Constitution as the supreme law of the land and mandated that all federal and state officers, including Supreme Court justices, should be bound by oath or affirmation to support the Constitution.

The Founding Fathers undertook to immunize Supreme Court justices against temptation to violate their oaths or affirmations to support the Constitution by making them independent of everything except the Constitution itself. To this end, they stipulated in Article III that Supreme Court justices "shall hold their offices during good behaviour . . . and receive for their services a compensation, which shall not be diminished during their continuance in office."

In commenting upon the obligation of Supreme Court justices to check unconstitutional action in his dissenting opinion in *United States v. Butler,* Justice (afterwards Chief Justice) Stone made this cogent comment: "While unconstitutional exercise of power by the executive and legislative branches of government is subject to judicial restraint, the only check upon our own exercise of power is our own sense of self-restraint."

Some exceedingly wise Americans, who understood and

revered the Constitution, have expressed opinions concerning
justices who do not exercise the self-restraint which their
oaths or affirmations to support the Constitution, impose
upon them, and the impact of their derelictions upon constitutional government.

George Washington, who served as president of the convention that framed the Constitution before becoming our
first President under it, gave America this solemn warning in
his *Farewell Address:*

> If in the opinion of the people, the distribution or modification
> of the constitutional powers be in any particular wrong, let it be
> corrected by an amendment in the way which the constitution
> designates. But let there be no change by usurpation; for though
> this, in one instance, may be the instrument of good, it is the cus-
> tomary weapon by which free governments are destroyed. The
> precedent must always overbalance in permanent evil any partial
> or transient benefit which the use can at any time yield.

Chief Justice Marshall emphasized the supreme importance of a Supreme Court justice accepting the Constitution
as the absolute rule for the government of his official conduct
by declaring that if he does not discharge his duties agreeably
to the Constitution his oath or affirmation to support that instrument "is worse than solemn mockery."

Another great constitutional scholar, Judge Thomas M.
Cooley, asserted that such a justice is "justly chargeable with
reckless disregard of official oath and public duty."

Benjamin N. Cardozo, Chief Judge of the New York Court
of Appeals and Justice of the United States Supreme Court,
stated in *The Nature of the Judicial Process* that "judges are
not commissioned to make and unmake rules at pleasure in
accordance with changing views of expediency or wisdom"
and that "it would put an end to the reign of law" if judges
adopted the practice of substituting their personal notions of
justice for rules established by a government of laws.

No question is more crucial to America than this: What
obligation does the Constitution impose upon Supreme Court
justices?

America's greatest jurist of all time, Chief Justice John

Marshall, answered this question with candor and clarity in his opinions in *Marbury v. Madison* and *Gibbons v. Ogden.* In these indisputably sound opinions, Chief Justice Marshall declared:

1. That the principles of the Constitution are designed to be permanent.
2. That the words of the Constitution must be understood to mean what they say.
3. That the Constitution constitutes an absolute rule for the government of Supreme Court Justices in their official action.

In elaborating the second declaration, Marshall said:

As men whose intentions require no concealment generally employ the words which most directly and aptly express the ideas they intend to convey, the enlightened patriots who framed our Constitution, and the people who adopted it, must be understood to have employed words in their natural sense, and to have intended what they have said.

Judges who perpetrate *verbicide* on the Constitution are judicial activists. A judicial activist is a judge who interprets the Constitution to mean what it would have said if he instead of the Founding Fathers had written it.

Contrary to popular opinion, all judicial activists are not liberals. Some of them are conservatives. A liberal judicial activist is a judge who expands the scope of the Constitution by stretching its words beyond their true meaning and a conservative judicial activist is one who narrows the scope of the Constitution by restricting their true meaning.

Judicial activism of the right or the left substitutes the personal will of the judge for the impersonal will of the law.

The majority opinion in *Miranda v. Arizona* is the product of liberal judicial activism and the majority opinion in *Laird v. Tatum* is the product of conservative judicial activism.

Judges are fallible human beings. The temptation to substitute one's personal notions of justice for law lies in wait for all occupants of judicial offices and sometimes ordinarily self-restrained judges succumb to it.

Nobody doubts the good intentions of the judicial activists. They undoubtedly lay the flattering unction to their souls that their judicial activism is better than the handiwork of the Founding Fathers and that America will be highly blessed by an exchange of the constitutional government ordained by the Constitution for a government embodying their personal notions.

Before accepting these assurances as verity Americans would do well to ponder what Daniel Webster said about public officials who undertake to substitute their good intentions for rules of law. Webster said:

Good intentions will always be pleaded for every assumption of authority. It is hardly too strong to say that the Constitution was made to guard the people against the dangers of good intentions. There are men in all ages who mean to govern well, but they mean to govern. They promise to be good masters, but they mean to be masters.

When the Constitutional Convention of 1787 submitted the Constitution to the states, Eldridge Gerry, who had been a delegate from Massachusetts, and George Mason, who had been a delegate from Virginia, opposed its ratification because it contained no provision sufficient to compel Supreme Court justices to obey their oaths or affirmations to support it.

Gerry complained that, "There are not well-defined limits to the judiciary powers" and that "it would be a herculean labour to attempt to describe the dangers with which they are replete."

George Mason said that "the power of construing the laws would enable the Supreme Court of the United States to substitute its own pleasure for the law of the land and that the errors and usurpations of the Supreme Court would be uncontrollable and remediless."

Alexander Hamilton, a delegate from New York, rejected these arguments with the emphatic assertion that "the supposed danger of judiciary encroachments . . . is, in reality, a phantom."

To support his assertion, Hamilton maintained in much detail that men selected to sit on the Supreme Court would be chosen with a view to those qualifications which fit men for the stations of judges and that they would give that inflexible and uniform adherence to legal rules and precedents which is indispensable in courts of justice.

By his remarks, Hamilton assured the several states that men selected to sit upon the Supreme Court would be able and willing to subject themselves to the restraint inherent in the judicial process.

Experience makes this proposition indisputable: Although one may possess a brilliant intellect and be actuated by lofty motives, he is not qualified for the station of judge in a government of laws unless he is able and willing to subject himself to the restraint inherent in the judicial process.

Hamilton's prediction about the qualifications of the men to be selected to serve as Supreme Court justices proved valid for generations. Unfortunately, however, for constitutional government in America, Hamilton's phantom has now become an exceedingly live ghost.

While they have acted with reasonable judicial decorum in ordinary cases, the tragic truth is that during recent years some Supreme Court justices have adopted and exercised the role of judicial activists with more or less abandon in cases involving the place of the states in the federal system, cases involving prosecution for crimes in federal and state courts and cases having emotional, political, and racial overtones.

A high proportion of these cases have been decided by a sharply divided court. Limitations of language and time compel me to confine my remarks in respect to them to the handiwork of the Supreme Court justices who have enacted the role of judicial activists and to omit reference to that of their brethren whose vigorous dissents have protested such actions.

By committing verbicide on the Constitution, the judicial activists concentrate in the federal government powers the Constitution reserves to the states; diminish the capacity of federal executive officers and the states to bring criminals to justice; rob individuals of personal and property rights; and expand their own powers and those of Congress far beyond their constitutional limits.

In Milton's poetic phrase, the cases in which the Supreme Court has committed *verbicide* upon the Constitution have become as "thick as autumnal leaves that strow the brooks of Vallombrosa."

The number and variety of these cases make it impossible to detail them within appropriate limits. If anyone should detail them in their entirety, he would be justly chargeable with forsaking time and encroaching upon eternity.

Merely to indicate how judicial verbicide performs its wonders, I cite a few of the innovative decisions an activist Supreme Court has handed down since 1968. They are *Jones v. Alfred H. Mayer Co.*, 392 U.S. 409; *Sullivan v. Little Hunting Park*, 396 U.S. 229; *Tillman v. Wheaton-Haven Recreation Association*, 410 U.S. 431; *Johnson v. Railway Express Agency*, 421 U.S. 454; *Runyon v. McCrary*, 427 U.S. 160; and *McDonald v. Santa Fe Trail Transportation Company*, 427 U.S. 273.

By committing colossal verbicide on the plain words of the Thirteenth Amendment and the Civil Rights Act of 1866, Supreme Court justices have assigned to themselves and Congress powers to dominate and punish the private thoughts, the private prejudices, and the private business and social activities of Americans which are repugnant to the powers given them by the Constitution.

In charging in Chief Justice John Marshall's unhappy phrase that some Supreme Court justices are making a solemn mockery of their oaths to support the Constitution, I am not a lone voice crying in a constitutional wilderness. I am, in truth, simply one member of a constantly expanding chorus.

Judge Learned Hand, Alexander Bickel, Philip B. Kurland, and other profoundly enlightened constitutional scholars have made similar accusations. These charges are corroborated in detail by these recent books: *Government By Judiciary*, by Raoul Berger; *The Price of Perfect Justice*, by Macklin Fleming; and *Disaster By Decree*, by Lino A. Graglia. Besides the apostacy of the activist justices to the Constitution is highlighted in numerous vigorous dissents by their brethren on the Supreme Court bench.

One of the most lucid comments on the judicial verbicide of activist Supreme Court Justices is that of Justice Jackson in his concurring opinion in *Brown v. Allen,* 344 U.S. 443, 542-550. In deploring the perverted use of the great writ of habeas corpus to rob the verdicts and judgments of state courts in criminal trials of any finality, Justice Jackson said:

Rightly or wrongly, the belief is widely held by the practicing profession that this Court no longer respects impersonal rules of law but is guided in these matters by personal impressions which from time to time may be shared by a majority of the Justices. Whatever has been intended, this Court also has generated an impression in much of the judiciary that regard for precedents and authorities is obsolete, that words no longer mean what they have always meant to the profession, that the law knows no fixed principles.

Justice Jackson closed his observations on judicial verbicide with this sage comment: "I know of no way we can have equal justice under law except we have some law."

Candor compels the confession that many Americans commend the usurpations of the activist Justices, especially when they harmonize with their wishes.

These erring ones seek to coerce critics of judicial activism into silence. To this end, they assert that all Supreme Court decisions are entitled to respect, and that those who criticize any of them are unpatriotic.

This assertion is contemptuous of the wisdom of the Founding Fathers in incorporating in the First Amendment for the benefit of all Americans guarantees of freedom of speech and the press. Besides, it is downright silly.

Like other official action, judicial decisions merit respect only when they are respectable, and no decision of the Supreme Court is respectable if it flouts the Constitution its makers have obligated themselves by oath or affirmation to support.

As Justice Felix Frankfurter so rightly declared: "Judges as persons, or courts as institutions, are entitled to no greater immunity from criticism than other persons or institutions. . . . Judges must be kept mindful of their limitations and their ultimate public responsibility by a vigorous stream of criticism expressed with candor however blunt."

Chief Justice Stone concurred with Justice Frankfurter's

view by stating that "where the courts deal, as ours do, with great public questions, the only protection against unwise decisions, and even judicial usurpation, is careful scrutiny of their action, and fearless comment upon it."

Apologists for the *verbicial* attacks of Supreme Court Justices upon the Constitution attempt to justify them by these arguments:

1. They are necessary to keep government abreast of the time because the amendatory process established by Article V is too cumbersome and dilatory.

2. They are desirable because they make pleasing amendments to the nation's supreme law which Congress and the states are unwilling to make.

3. They prove that the Constitution is a living instrument of government.

There are two incontestable answers to these arguments in their entirety. They are first, that tyranny on the bench is as reprehensible as tyranny on the throne; and, second, that the ultimate result of judicial activism on the part of the Supreme Court justices is the destruction of the government of laws the Constitution was ordained by the people to create and preserve.

There are also separate irrefutable answers to each of the arguments.

As James Madison, the father of the Constitution, stated, the Founding Fathers created the amendatory process of which the apologists complain to ensure that Congress and the states will act with deliberation when they consider proposed changes in the Constitution and will refrain from acting unwisely in making them.

The Founding Fathers knew that a constitution is destitute of value if its provisions are as mutable as simple legislative enactments, and they certainly did not intend that decisions of constitutional questions by the Supreme Court should ever be rightly compared as they were by Justice Roberts in a colorful phase with restricted railroad tickets, good for this day and train only.

The second argument of the apologists is the stuff of

which tyranny is made. Its underlying premise is their apprehension that Congress and the states acting in combination may have too much wisdom to amend the Constitution in ways pleasing to them. Hence, they maintain that for their pleasure Supreme Court justices ought to usurp and exercise the power the Constitution vests exclusively in the people to have the Constitution amended only by the representatives they choose to act for them at congressional and state levels.

The usurpation of this power by Supreme Court justices does not prove that the Constitution is a living instrument of government. On the contrary, it proves that the Constitution is dead and that the people of our land are being ruled by the transitory personal notions of justices who occupy for a fleeting moment of history seats on the Supreme Court bench rather than by the enduring precepts of the Constitution.

Despite Miranda's disapproval of confessions, I am going to make an honest one.

Those who abhor tyranny on the bench as much as tyranny on the throne are unable to devise any pragmatic procedure to compel activist judges to observe their oaths or affirmations to support the Constitution.

Judicial aberrations are not impeachable offenses under Article II, Section 4. No earthly power can compel activist justices to exercise self-restraint if they are unable or unwilling to do so, and the soundest criticism is not likely to deter activist justices from their activism and verbicide when they honestly believe their handiwork is better than that of the Founding Fathers. It is obvious, moreover, that Congress and the states cannot protect constitutional government adequately by adding new amendments to the Constitution. This is true for these reasons: First, it is folly to expect activist justices to obey new constitutional provisions when they spurn the old; and, second, it would complicate simplicity and convert the Constitution into a confusing document as long as the *Encyclopaedia Britannica* to rid us of all the judicial usurpations of recent years.

All history proclaims this everlasting truth: No nation can enjoy the right to self-rule and the right to freedom from tyranny under a government of men. The Founding Fathers framed and ratified the Constitution to secure these precious rights to Americans for all time.

Judicial verbicide substitutes the personal notions of judges for the precepts of the Constitution. Hence, judicial verbicide is calculated to convert the Constitution into a worthless scrap of paper and to replace our government of laws with a judicial oligarchy.

A great senator, Daniel Webster, warned America in eloquent words what the destruction of our Constitution would entail. He said:

Other misfortunes may be borne, or their effects overcome. If disastrous wars should sweep our commerce from the ocean, another generation may renew it; if it exhaust our treasury, future industry may replenish it; if it desolate and lay waste our fields, still, under a new cultivation, they will grow green again, and ripen to future harvests.

It were but a trifle even if the walls of yonder Capitol were to crumble, if its lofty pillars should fall, and its gorgeous decorations be all covered by the dust of the valley. All of these may be rebuilt.

But who shall reconstruct the fabric of demolished government?

Who shall read again the well-proportioned columns of constitutional liberty?

Who shall frame together the skillful architecture which unites national sovereignty with state rights, individual security, and public prosperity?

No, if these columns fall, they will be raised not again. Like the Colisseum and the Parthenon, they will be destined to a mournful and melancholy immortality. Bitterer tears, however, will flow over them than ever were shed over the monuments of Roman or Grecian art; for they will be the monuments of a more glorious edifice than Greece or Rome ever saw—the edifice of constitutional American Liberty.

In closing, I reiterate some inescapable conclusions.

The distinction between the power to amend the Constitution and the power to interpret it is as wide as the gulf which yawns between Lazarus in Abraham's bosom and Dives in hell. The power to amend is the power to change the meaning of the Constitution and the power to interpret is the power to determine the meaning of the Constitution as established by the Founding Fathers.

The Founding Fathers did not contemplate that any Supreme Court justice would convert his oath or affirmation to support the Constitution into something worse than solemn mockery. On the contrary, they contemplated that his oath or affirmation to support that supreme instrument of government would implant indelibly in his mind, heart, and conscience a solemn obligation to be faithful to the Constitution.

A justice who twists the words of the Constitution awry under the guise of interpreting it to substitute his personal notion for a constitutional precept is contemptuous of intellectual integrity. His act in so doing is as inexcusable as that of the witness who commits perjury after taking an oath or making an affirmation to testify truthfully.

We must not despair because there is no way by which law can compel activist Supreme Court justices to subject their personal wills to the precepts of the Constitution.

This is true because it is not yet unconstitutional for Americans to invoke divine aid when they are at their wits' end.

Hence, we can pray—hopefully not in vain—that the activist Justices will heed the tragic truth spoken by Webster and their own oaths or affirmations to support the Constitution, and become born-again supporters of the most precious instrument of government the world has ever known.

TERRORISM: THE THREAT TO SECURITY

WELCOME HOME[1]

RONALD W. REAGAN[2]

In an emotion-charged ceremony on the South Lawn of the White House on the afternoon of Tuesday, January 27, 1981, President Ronald Reagan welcomed home the 52 Americans who had been held hostage in Iran for 444 days. The welcome by the President and response by former hostage L. Bruce Laingen climaxed one of the most emotional weeks in recent American history. Beginning a week earlier, Americans watched on television and followed in the news the departure of the former hostages from Teheran, their arrival in Algiers, the welcome by former President Jimmy Carter in Wiesbaden, their return to the United States, and their trip to the United States Military Academy at West Point, New York, where they were reunited with family and friends.

January 27 marked their first truly public appearance after their release. The day began with a group press conference at West Point. Then, accompanied by 400 relatives, the 52 released hostages flew to Washington in four Air Force planes. From the time the first plane touched down until the end of the ceremony on the White House lawn at 3:25 P.M., an estimated 265,000 Washington residents and visitors who turned out and millions of Americans who watched on television saw the returning Americans in their triumphal trip through the Capital. Reporter Howell Raines described the event:

> Even in a city used to heroes and ceremony, this day was judged something extraordinary. That became clear as the motorcade swung over an Anacostia River bridge to the spontaneous whooping of sirens, the streaming arcs of water from the fireboats, and the steadily growing crowds along the sidewalks. As the buses approached the White House along Pennsylvania Avenue, the crowds surged forward to touch the vehicles and

[1] Delivered on the South Lawn of the White House, Washington, D.C., at approximately 3 P.M. on January 27, 1981.
[2] For biographical note, see Appendix.

people wept openly. "It's the most emotional experience of our lives," said Mr. [Vice President] Bush. "You could feel it build until the point it hurt inside. It was the greatest event I've ever seen."

And at every turn, the town was bedecked with yellow ribbon, from the public buses to the storefronts, from the spectators' lapels to the school in northwest Washington, where the children spent the morning lacing ribbons into the school fence. (New York *Times*, Ja. 28, '81, p 1)

After a private reception in the Blue Room, the President and former hostages emerged from the White House to a platform on the South Lawn to the accompaniment of ruffles and flourishes of a military band. Assembled on the lawn were 6,000 invited government dignitaries and employees. Following an invocation and military salute, President Reagan delivered his welcome. Released hostage L. Bruce Laingen, former chargé d'affaires at the United States Embassy in Teheran, responded for the returning Americans.

In planning the event, according to Richard J. Cattani, President Reagan wanted a personal, constrained ceremony, but at the same time he and his advisers recognized the role such presidential rituals play in unifying and refreshing the national spirit—"like an inauguration marking an orderly end of one era and a fresh, hopeful start." (*Christian Science Monitor*, Ja. 28, '81, p 1)

New York *Times* writer Hedrick Smith described the event as follows:

> President Reagan chose a moment of enormous emotional fervor, a moment of national patriotic communion this afternoon to proclaim a resurgent and more assertive America willing to use force swiftly to protect its diplomats abroad. His sharp and unmistakable warning . . . was a deliberate gesture to try to make a break with the past. . . . Members of the Reagan circle said they were happy to inherit the surge of national pride and to ride into office on a crest of good feeling. (New York *Times*, Ja. 28, '81, p 11)

Hedrick also noted Reagan's shrewd sense of timing in deciding not to greet the former hostages immediately upon their return, but to allow time for a crescendo of excitement to build. He characterized the President's language as stern, sharp, and "vintage Reagan," echoing "hundreds of after-dinner speeches and campaign addresses in which he excoriated the diminution of American power abroad and urged a bolder protection of American interest."

Bruce Laingen, who replied for the freed hostages, is a career diplomat. In his response, Laingen, according to B. Drummond Ayres Jr., momentarily transfixed "a national television audience with his plucky humor, grace, dramatic eloquence and, above all, his devotion to family and country."

It may have been the ultimate diplomatic act for Mr. Laingen, a 30-year veteran of the Foreign Service, who remains boyishly handsome despite being 58 years old and having spent the last 15 months under great pressure. As he spoke at the White House of "the best qualities of our people" and of the former hostages "who will always have a love affair with this country," an unmistakable look of pride, even satisfaction, filled the faces of the surrounding crowd of officials and visitors. Tears welled in the eyes of President Reagan.

Mr. Laingen's friends at the State Department were moved by his appearance on the South Lawn, but not surprised. "Everything he's ever touched," one longtime colleague commented, "has been handled in a deft, smooth, extremely professional manner. He's an idealistic, dedicated career servant, and the welfare of his country is what his life is all about." (New York *Times*, Ja. 28, '81, p 9)

The ceremonies surrounding the return of the hostages to this country were described as a national catharsis, something the United States had been seeking for a long time and finally got, and a "ceremonial beginning and ending," like christenings and funerals. One observer said, "I looked at them and felt proud to be an American, and I haven't had precisely the same feeling since I was a little boy watching the troop ships come back to New Orleans from the Second World War." (New York *Times*, Ja. 28, '81, p 10)

In an editorial, the New York *Times* perhaps summed up the feeling in the country,

Now, the countryside is abloom in red, white, blue—and yellow ribbons; the air is filled with prayers and cheers, bells and bands. The festivities are as welcome as the occasion. The hostages are not all that has been returned to the United States. . . . Now, the pride and patriotism that many people tried to unfurl during the Bicentennial have erupted without embarrassment. It's not as though there are no more divisions in the country. . . . But on every side, there has suddenly ap-

peared a need to express national unity, to demonstrate an un-
ashamed patriotism. The hostages say they never expected
such a welcome. How could they? They have returned to a different country than the one they knew only 14 months ago.
(New York *Times*, Ja. 27, '81, p 22)

Thank you. Thank you again. Cardinal Cooke, thank you,
I think, for delivering this weather. We had been promised showers; we're most grateful. Welcome to the ambassa-
dors of our friends and neighboring countries who are here
today.

And I can think of no better way to let you know how
Nancy and I feel about your presence here today than to say on
behalf of us, of the Vice President and Barbara, the senators,
the members of Congress, the members of the Cabinet and
all of our fellow citizens, these simple words: Welcome home.

You'll be seated, please. You are home. And believe me,
you're welcome.

If my remarks were a sermon, my text would be lines from
the 126th Psalm: "We were like those who dream. Now our
mouth is filled with laughter and our tongue with shouts of
joy. The Lord has done great things for us. We are glad."

You've come home to a people who for 444 days suffered
the pain of your imprisonment, prayed for your safety and,
most importantly, shared your determination that the spirit of
free men and women is not a fit subject for barter.

You've represented under great stress the highest traditions of public service. Your conduct is symbolic of the millions of professional diplomats, military personnel and others
who have rendered service to their country.

We're now aware of the conditions under which you were
imprisoned. Though now is not the time to review every ab-
horrent detail of your cruel confinement, believe me, we
know what happened. Truth may be a rare commodity today
in Iran; it's alive and well in America.

By no choice of your own, you've entered the ranks of
those who throughout our history have undergone the ordeal
of imprisonment. The crew of the Pueblo, the prisoners in
two World Wars, and in Korea and Vietnam. And like those
others, you are special to us.

You fulfilled your duty as you saw it. And now, like the others, thank God, you're home, and our hearts are full of gratitude.

I'm told that Sergeant Lopez here put up a sign in his cell, a sign that normally would have been torn down by those guards. But this one was written in Spanish, and his guards didn't know that *Viva la roja, blanca y azul* means "Long live the red, white and blue."

They may not understand what that means in Iran, but we do, Sergeant Lopez. And you've filled our hearts with pride. *Muchas gracias.*

Two days ago Nancy and I met with your families here at the White House. We know that you were lonely during that dreadful period of captivity, but you were never alone. Your wives and children, your mothers and dads, your brothers and sisters were so full of prayers and love for you that whether you were conscious of it or not, it must have sustained you during some of the worst times. No power on earth could prevent them from doing that.

Their courage, endurance, and strength were of heroic measure, and they're admired by all of us.

But to get down now to more mundane things—in case you have a question about your personal futures, you'll probably have less time to rest than you'd like. While you were on your way to Germany, I signed a hiring freeze in the Federal Government. In other words, we need you, your country needs you, and your bosses are panting to have you back on the job.

Now, I'll not be so foolish as to say forget what you've been through; you never will. But turn the page and look ahead. And do so knowing that for all who serve their country, whether in the foreign service, the military or as private citizens, freedom is indivisible. Your freedom and your individual dignity are much cherished.

Those henceforth in the representation of this nation will be accorded every means of protection that America can offer. Let terrorists be aware that when the rules of international behavior are violated, our policy will be one of swift and effective retribution.

We hear it said that we live in an era of limit to our powers. Well, let it also be understood, there are limits to our patience.

Now I'm sure that you'll want to know that with us here today are families of the eight heroic men who gave their lives in the attempt to effect your rescue. Greater glory hath no man than that he lay down his life for another.

And with us also are Colonel Beckwith and some of the men who did return from that mission. We ask God's special healing for those who suffered wounds and discomfort, to those who lost loved ones. To them, to you and to your families, again, welcome from all America. And thank you for making us proud to be Americans.

And now, ladies and gentlemen, I call on, to speak for this wonderful group of returnees, Bruce Laingen, deputy chief of mission in Teheran. Mr. Laingen.

L. Bruce Laingen[2]

Mr. President, Mrs. Reagan, members of the Cabinet, Vice President and Mrs. Bush—I think I've got that out of order of priority in protocol terms—members of the diplomatic corps who are here, and all you beautiful people out there, I'm not sure I'm capable of this, after that emotionally draining but beautiful experience that all of us have just had on the streets of this magnificent city.

Mr. President, I hope you were watching TV because I don't think any of us Americans have ever seen anything quite like it, quite so spontaneous, quite so beautiful, in terms of the best qualities of our people. And we are deeply grateful for it.

Mr. President, our flight to freedom is now complete, thanks to the prayers and good will of countless millions of people, not just in this country but all around the world; and the assistance of those many countries and governments who understood the values and principles that were at stake in this crisis; and the love and affection of our countrymen from all those tens of thousands out there on the streets today, to that lady that we saw standing on a hillside as we came in from

Andrews, all alone with no sign, no one around her, holding her hand to her heart; the enveloping love and affection of small-town America of the kind we witnessed in that wonderful two-day stop in New York State—West Point and its environs; and last but not least this flight to freedom, the United States Air Force on Freedom One.

Mr. President, I give you now 52 Americans, supplemented by a 53d today—Richard Queen sitting over here—overjoyed in reunion with our families: the real heroes in this crisis.

Fifty-three Americans proud to rejoin their professional colleagues who had made this flight to freedom earlier: our six colleagues who came here with the great cooperation and friendship of our Canadian friends, and our 13 who came earlier.

I give you now 53 Americans proud, as I said earlier today, to record their undying respect and affection for the families of those brave eight men who gave their lives so that we might be free. The 53 of us proud today, this afternoon, also to see and to meet with some of those families, and Colonel Beckwith and some of those that came back; 53 Americans who will always have a love affair with this country, and who join with you in a prayer of thanksgiving for the way in which this crisis has strengthened the spirit and resilience and strength that is the mark of a true, truly free, society.

Mr. President, we've seen a lot of signs along the road, here and up in New York. They are marvelous signs, as is the spirit and enthusiasm that accompanies this, what we call, what we have been calling a celebration of freedom. They are signs that have not been ordered; they are spontaneous, sincere signs that reflect the true feelings of the hearts of those that hold them—even those, I suppose, like "I.R.S. Welcomes You," which we saw today as we came into town, and another one that said, "The Government Workers Welcome You Back to Work,"—well we're ready.

There was another sign that said—and I think that says it as well as any—the best, as far as we're concerned, "The Best Things in Life Are Free." But even better than that was a sign that we saw as we left West Point today, along a super highway up there that someone had hastily put up, "And the World Will Be Better for This." And we pray, Mr. President, that this will be so.

Mr. President, in very simple words that come from the hearts of all of us, it is good to be back. Thank you, America, and God bless all of you. Thank you very much.

REAGAN: Thank you. This is a flag, in this case bearing your name, and it is a symbol I will give to you now because all the others—you will each receive one when we get inside the building and each one of you will have a flag symbolic of the 53 that are here, in your honor.

And now—Nancy, come on up here, I think now a fit ending for all of this would be for all of us to participate in singing "God Bless America."

REAGAN: Good night. Thank you. God bless you.

TERRORISM AND LOW-LEVEL CONFLICTS: A CHALLENGE FOR THE 1980s[1]

ANTHONY C. E. QUAINTON[2]

For 444 days in 1980–1981 fifty-two Americans were held hostage in Iran. This event, as no other, focused the attention of the American public on the problem of international terrorism. Dr. Ernest Evans, scholar and specialist in the study of terrorism, believes that the number of international terrorist incidents is at an all-time high. According to Evans, "You don't find anything on this scale in history before. I suspect that part of this is because terrorists have learned how to exploit advanced technology—aircraft and communications. The big change now is that they have discovered the electronic media—ways to get publicity they never had before." In Evans' opinion, "it could become much worse in the years ahead." (*Christian Science Monitor,* Ap. 2, '81)

[1] Delivered at the annual convention of the American Society for Industrial Security in the East Ballroom of the Fontainebleu Hilton Hotel, Miami Beach Florida, at 10 A.M., September 25, 1980.
[2] For biographical note, see Appendix.

On September 25, 1980, Anthony C. E. Quainton, director of the Office for Combating Terrorism of the Department of State, delivered an outstanding speech on the subject of terrorism to the American Society for Industrial Security at its annual convention in Miami Beach, Florida. The speech is one of several he delivered on the subject at various conferences and meetings throughout the year.

Ambassador Quainton, who entered the Foreign Service in 1959, served in diplomatic positions in Australia, India, Pakistan, France, Nepal, and the Central African Empire before becoming Director of the Office for Combating Terrorism.

The American Society for Industrial Security is an organization with approximately 14,000 members, most of whom are officials in industry responsible for loss prevention security functions of their company and government officials employed in a professional capacity in security.

Ambassador Quainton presented his speech at a General Session of the ASIS convention at 10 A.M. to an audience of approximately 1,100 in the East Ballroom of the Fontainebleu Hilton Hotel in Miami Beach, Florida. The vast majority of those present were security personnel and members of the organization, although there were also some students, business executives, and press representatives in attendance. The speech was followed by a press conference.

The speech provides an excellent example of the effective use of statistics and the citing of specific instances to develop a speaker's arguments.

Violence abounds in our world. Governments and corporations are equally affected. The statistics for 1979 were horrendous: Worldwide, 293 major incidents including 47 assassinations, 20 kidnappings, 13 hostage-barricade situations, not to mention bombings and armed attacks. Seventy-seven of these terrorist incidents directly involved U.S. citizens or property. High on the list came the kidnapping and murder of our ambassador to Afghanistan in February, 1979, the seizure of our Embassy in Iran in November, and the killing of eight of our citizens in violent attacks in Turkey throughout the year.

The story for 1980 is even more alarming. In the first eight months alone, there have been 500 incidents, of which 101 have involved Americans. One American ambassador was taken hostage in Bogota and held for 61 days; another in Beirut narrowly escaped assassination a month ago. Americans have been kidnapped and held for ransom in Guatemala and Colombia. Overall, 58 countries have been the target of at least one attack. Even the Soviet Union, which many have thought to be immune, has had to face over 30 terrorist attacks putting it second in the listing of countries most frequently targeted. The United States, alas, remains in first place.

In 1979 and 1980, the private sector has been particularly hard hit. Let me cite the major incidents in 1979 of which I am aware which were directed against your corporations:

January 3—The General Manager of Texaco in Colombia killed, having been held hostage since the previous May.

February 13—The Cairo Sheraton bombed—17 people injured.

February 19—The Pan American office in Izmir, Turkey bombed.

April 19—Explosives detonated at the Ford Motor Company showroom in Valencia, Spain.

April 23—A subsidiary of Babcock and Wilcox bombed in Dusseldorf, Germany.

May 20—The IBM office in San Salvador strafed.

June 15—The Nicaraguan Manager of National Cash Register kidnapped in El Salvador.

June 20—An American Airlines jet hijacked to Ireland by a Serbian nationalist.

July 24—The offices of the Wells Fargo Bank in Istanbul, Turkey bombed.

August 14—The factory of Apex Textile Company seized in El Salvador, its American General Manager held for nine days.

September 21—Two American executives of Beckman Instruments kidnapped in El Salvador.

October 26/28—Citicorp's Deputy Manager shot to death; the Bank of America office bombed. Both in El Salvador.

November 26—Armenian terrorists bomb Western Airlines and TWA in Madrid.

December 3—Morgan Guarantee Trust in Frankfurt bombed.

December 5—W.R. Grace Fertilizer Plant in Trinidad bombed.

December 14—Three Boeing contract employees killed in Istanbul.

December 23—TWA bombed in Rome.

December 25—Citibank and ITT bombed in El Salvador.

In 1980, there has been no respite. In Trinidad a Texaco refinery was bombed; so were TWA offices in Madrid. A Texaco regional vice president was abducted in Honduras. A similar attempt was made against a Colgate Palmolive executive in Cali, Colombia. And in the last month, a series of bombings have damaged banks and other American corporation premises in Manila. Finally, the month of August enters into the Guinness book of terrorist records as the month with the most hijackings, all of American aircraft.

I have cited for you only some of the more dramatic incidents which have directly affected U.S. interests. I have not mentioned, for example, the Corsican terrorists' attempt to blow up an oil refinery near Marseilles or the successful attack against South Africa's major synthetic fuels manufacturing plant. These two incidents have a particular significance since they represent attacks on highly sensitive facilities, rather than the more traditional symbolic attacks on airline offices and banks.

In the last year we have also seen a new phenomenon—systematic assassinations by states of their political enemies abroad. Assassinations have succeeded in 24 countries with 23 different groups involved. The assassinations have included Libyans and Iraqis in Europe, Syrians in Jordan, Iranians in the United States, and most recently the killing of ex-President Somoza in Paraguay. The international community is faced with a growing lawlessness, a diminishing respect for international law, a continuing erosion of the basic principles of diplomatic intercourse. There is no reason to suppose that these attacks will stop. We must anticipate increasing numbers of violent acts as the 80s advance.

What we did not see in the 1970s was any significant escalation of terrorist tactics. To be sure, in the last two years there have been more casualties than ever before. But the terrorists continue to kill with relatively unsophisticated weapons: homemade bombs, automatic weapons, and rocket propelled grenades. We have seen no evidence that terrorists are about to turn to esoteric weapons (nuclear, chemical or biological), recent novels such as the *Fifth Horseman* notwithstanding.

There are, however, some indications that we may see a change to new and more significant targets. If so, the private sector will be directly affected. It is evident to most of us that in modern society there are numerous vulnerabilities: computers, power generation and transmission systems, tankers, off-shore oil facilities, etc. Many of these are only lightly protected. Security for these installations will require the most careful attention in the years ahead and the closest possible cooperation between government and industry. The cost will be high.

I have attended several conferences in the last six months at which these issues have been discussed and at which industry and government representatives have begun to examine together ways in which we can address the next generation of problems. At this point in time, we cannot predict with any certainty which facilities or which industries are most likely to be attacked or threatened. However, given the high stakes and the potential costs of being unprepared, we must be sure that the best minds available are doing the contingency planning which is needed.

But before returning to the question of what needs to be done in the future, let me review for you what we have already achieved. In the last five years, we have developed a strategy for combating terrorism and other forms of low-level violence which has five elements: intelligence, physical security, contingency planning, crisis management, and international cooperation. None of these is new; all have been significantly improved and upgraded in recent years. In the crucible of events our competence has been refined. We have learned a number of lessons which should stand us in good stead as we approach the 21st century.

In some ways the most important lesson is that intelligence in the broadest sense is critical. Ten years ago we knew little about terrorist groups, their leaders or their *modus operandi*. This situation has dramatically changed, notwithstanding self-imposed restraints on some kinds of intelligence activity. We now do have computer data bases which enable us rapidly to factor information about terrorist groups into our crisis management system.

Most significantly we have information about terrorist plans. Almost every week somewhere in the world we are informed of a specific threat against one of our diplomats or embassies or against a private corporation, airline, or executive. Without exception, this information is passed to our embassies through diplomatic channels, or in the case of the private sector, through the State Department's Office of Security to the corporation concerned. Intelligence is worthless if it is not used. It is a highly perishable commodity. Although we must be concerned to protect sensitive sources and methods, I can assure you whenever we are aware of information which affects the security of your companies or your executives, you will be the first to know.

Unfortunately, intelligence provides only a partial answer. We will not have forewarning of all terrorist attacks. The problems of penetrating small, highly dedicated terrorist cells are enormous. The resources available are limited. We must therefore take other measures to deter attacks. The most obvious of which is physical security. I do not pretend to be an expert in this field, and certainly with so much talent and expertise in the audience, I am hesitant to offer any guidance. Nonetheless, I am convinced that security does pay off. Our ambassador in Beirut was saved in an assassination attempt last month because he was in a specially protected vehicle and had armed and trained professional security officers with him. Our embassy and ambassador's residence in Bogota were not attacked this spring because the M-19 concluded that the protective systems in place were too difficult to breach. They chose the Dominican Republic Embassy instead. Only once, in fact, in Kuala Lumpur in 1976 has an American embassy been taken over by a terrorist group. Everywhere else terrorists have been successfully deterred.

Unfortunately, the systems created to deter the entry of terrorists were insufficient to deal with the mob violence which we saw in Pakistan, Iran, and Libya in the last year. We are now embarked on a major upgrading of our embassy security at a cost of over $40 million to improve perimeter controls and to develop the concept of internal safe-havens. We must give our personnel abroad the protection which they need in a world of growing violence and in which governments may be unable or unwilling to come to our assistance promptly. No task has a higher priority for our security experts in the department.

In the last decade we have also made notable progress in deterring hijackings. With almost 20,000 weapons seized at American airports since 1974, we know that the system works. Only one plane in all that time has been hijacked in the United States with a weapon taken through screening. Now we are faced with a new weapon: flammable liquid. Improved screening methods will have to be devised. The FAA is already actively engaged in seeking a solution to this new threat.

We all know that security is only as good as its weakest link. We, as you, must be alert to any weaknesses so that we can enhance our protective systems and thereby diminish the vulnerability of those we are called on to protect. But weaknesses there will always be, and we must assume that occasionally terrorists will succeed in taking hostages or in carrying out some other violent act. When terrorists succeed, we must be prepared with adequate contingency plans and a crisis management structure that ensures that all appropriate resources are rapidly deployed toward the resolution of the incident.

We have given high priority to contingency planning. Every American embassy and consulate is required to have plans to cover bomb threats, internal defense, hijackings and hostage incidents. Every FBI field office in the United States has plans for handling terrorist incidents in collaboration with appropriate local law enforcement agencies. The Federal Government has a National Response Plan for Nuclear Emergencies including terrorist attacks. There now exists a credibility assessment system for all kinds of nuclear and other esoteric threats. Within hours through this system the Federal Government can obtain a succinct and technically sound appraisal of any threat received. We are looking as a priority at ways to improve our contingency plans for handling incidents in the maritime environment. The Counter-Terrorist Joint Task Force which the Department of Defense is creating as a result of Admiral Holloway's report, will provide yet another level of contingency preparedness. The purpose of all of these plans and preparations is to make certain that we have ready and clearly defined lines of command and control and the necessary supporting resources, including communications, which we will need to manage a crisis.

Plans only provide a framework within which crisis managers can act. They do not provide policy guidelines nor ensure the harmonious working of a system which ultimately depends on the personal relations which exist among representatives of various agencies and jurisdictions. In recent years we have worked to build experienced teams of area and intelligence experts, behavioral scientists, security professionals, public relations officers. They are used to working together. They understand the basic policy framework in which they must act. They have training in the basic principles of hostage negotiation and crisis management. When there are major policy issues to be addressed in the course of an incident, they are taken promptly to the Special Coordination Committee of the National Security Council. The SCC is the policy level group to which the Working Group on Terrorism and its Executive Committee report for guidance. Similarly, the lead agency responsible for managing an incident (the FBI/Justice domestically, the State Department abroad, the FAA in the case of hijackings) would also get its guidance from the SCC.

As part of our preparation for future terrorist attacks, we have given high priority to the training of all employees of all Federal Government agencies serving abroad. At the Foreign Service Institute in Washington we offer a course on terrorism and coping with violence which provides an introduction to such subjects as surveillance recognition, travel precautions and countering vehicular kidnapping, recognition of and defenses against letter and parcel bombs, residential security, protection against local crime, preparedness for riots and demonstrations, preparation for family separations and evacuations, and hostage survival. We are now paying particular attention to the needs of families; for our experience has been that they must be part of any emergency planning system. Spouses and other adult family members attend all our counter-terrorist and security training courses.

Increasingly, in our contingency planning and crisis management we have come to recognize that no one agency has all the answers. Crisis management is a team effort in which many agencies and many layers of state and local government are involved. In more and more incidents, the private sector is an essential element of this partnership. In hijackings the airline concerned is always a part of the government crisis network sharing in the decisions and listening and contributing to the analysis of the evolving situation. Similar structures may be needed in the future if we are faced with other kinds of terrorist attacks or hostage incidents involving corporate assets and personnel.

Because of the need for close cooperation, we must face squarely the fact that we do not always agree. In some terrorist incidents, the government and private industry may have conflicting interests, priorities and policies. For example, industry usually pays ransom: the government does not. Yet both are concerned for the lives at stake in the immediate situation and for the possibility that others will be at risk in the future. Both should be aware of the political radicalization which may result from giving in to terrorist demands. To the extent that ransom fuels the coffers of revolutionary groups, long-term government and corporate interests may suffer. On these issues we need to have a more vigorous dialogue so that each side understands the rationale for the other's policy and the problems which may result from different corporate and government strategies. I hope and believe that these differences can be minimized so that when we are faced with an actual incident we will be working together rather than at cross purposes.

The final aspect of our strategy for dealing with terrorism and its proliferation is international cooperation. Here too we have made progress although not as much as we would have liked. On a number of fronts the international community has demonstrated that it agrees with us that there are certain kinds of terrorist acts which are inadmissible in civilized society and which are contrary to the basic principles of international law. These include aircraft hijacking and sabotage, attacks on diplomats and the taking of hostages. All of these acts are now covered by international conventions drawn up in the 1970s. The most recent is the Convention Against the Taking of Hostages which was opened for signature last December and which the United States signed almost immediately thereafter. This Convention is before the Senate for ratification.

All of the Conventions impose upon states party to them the obligation either to prosecute or extradite the perpetrators of these crimes. Unfortunately, not all crimes are covered by conventions: assassinations, bombings, vessel hijackings are still outside this system of universal condemnation. In addition, none of the Conventions provides for enforcement measures against states which violate their obligations as Iran did so flagrantly in the seizure of American hostages last November. The only exception is the undertaking of seven leading aviation nations to cut-off air services to countries which harbor hijackers. The Bonn Declaration, as it is known, marks a significant turning point in international attitudes. We hope it will be extended to other areas, but we are realistic enough to realize that this process may take time and that some states will refuse to accept the limitations on their sovereignty which any system of sanctions implies.

As we look ahead to the last two decades of this century, we will undoubtedly see high levels of violence and turmoil. Increasing population pressures, growing competition for scarce resources, widening income disparities within and between societies will create uncertainty and lead to various forms of conflict. Some of the turbulence in the world will take the form of traditional terrorism—hostage taking, kidnapping, etc. Some will be in the form of urban unrest, revolution, and civil war. We must also anticipate continuing incidents of state-supported violence and terrorism. This phenomenon of state violence exercised through surrogate groups may, in fact, become one of the major political issues of the 1980s.

Nonetheless, high though the levels of violence may be, we need not despair. Government and the private sector have coped with violence in the past and can do so in the future. However, if we are to succeed, we will have to refine the tools which we have already identified—intelligence, security, crisis management, contingency planning, international cooperation.

Above all else, we must develop sound working relationships between government and industry. A close partnership is essential. Of especial importance will be research and development into techniques which will deter terrorists, protect executives, and deflect threats. One area which is already of great importance is the technological frontier represented by explosive taggants. Within the next decade we will be able to add to explosive materials both detection and identification taggants permitting us to spot bombs before they go off and to track down the perpetrators afterwards. This technology is of particular significance given the fact that bombs still represent the most numerous and most serious threat that we face. I have no reason to suppose that that situation will change in the years ahead.

If we are to cooperate more effectively, as I believe we

must, we have to understand each other better and know where and how to get the information we need. This Convention is enormously valuable in bringing together so many professional security experts for a detailed exchange of views, information, and technology. ASIS makes a unique contribution to this process through its terrorism committee and its regional seminars.

In Washington, there is unfortunately no central point for information or assistance. However, I would like to commend to you a small pamphlet which the Department of Commerce has recently put out entitled *Combatting Terrorism: Sources of Federal Assistance for Business.* It describes a number of places you can go for assistance and the kinds of help which are available. I know I speak for my colleagues at State, Commerce, the FBI, FAA, and Defense in saying that one of our principal responsibilities is to support and collaborate with the private sector. We need to know your concerns and your problems. We welcome the contact which meetings such as this provide. For they are sure signs of that spirit of partnership through which we can jointly meet the challenges of terrorism and low-level conflict in the 1980s.

THE MEDIA

INTERNATIONAL COMMUNICATIONS: THE IMPACT OF THE MASS MEDIA[1]

James W. Carey[2]

Noting that, "For the first time since the 1950s the structure of social communication throughout much of the world has been radically destabilized," James W. Carey in a speech on April 29, 1980, sought to explain and predict the consequences of this changing technology and its implications for the flow of international communication in the future.

Dean of the College of Communications at the University of Illinois, author of many articles, and popular lecturer, the speaker is recognized as a scholar in the fields of communication, mass media, and popular culture.

Dr. Carey delivered his speech at a Fulbright Commission meeting at the University of Illinois. He presented it to a symposium of former Fulbright scholars who were at the time working in the United States at the Levis Faculty Center of the University of Illinois in Urbana at 8 o'clock in the evening. Dr. Carey's audience of approximately 150 persons included Fulbright scholars, former Fulbright scholars then on the University of Illinois faculty, members of the university administration, and other interested faculty and students.

The speech was preceded by a dinner and the opening ceremonies of the conference, a welcome by the university chancellor, and an introduction from the university and the International Communications Agency.

I am honored to be speaking to this conference of distinguished international scholars and no less honored to be part of a program, now almost thirty-five years old, designed to promote not only international understanding but the diffu-

---

[1] Delivered at a meeting of the Fulbright Commission at the Levis Faculty Center of the University of Illinois in Urbana at 8 P.M. on April 29, 1980.

[2] For biographical note, see Appendix.

sion of scholarship and cooperative intelligence on the broadest possible scale.

But, if honored, I am also wary for I received a difficult, indeed treacherous assignment. The range of disciplines, countries, and cultures represented here make it impossible to readily find some common language of discourse. Moreover, international communications is a subject about which we can all claim to be experts by our very participation in the Fulbright program. Finally, the United States is, in terms of international communication, an anomalous country and an American is not the ideal person to treat this topic. We are major exporters of communication to the rest of the world but, unlike most other exporters, we are not major importers of the culture and communications of other people. We inevitably see the problems of international communications from a narrow and biased perspective. Despite those limitations, allow me some reflections on the consequences of changing communication technology for international communication.

For the first time since the 1950s the structure of social communication throughout much of the world has been radically destabilized. In turn this destabilization has consequences for the flow of international communication.

Lying behind this destabilization are two major technical innovations. First, satellite broadcasting, which for purposes of communication puts everyone in the same place or, inversely, eliminates distance as a cost factor in communications; and second, computer technology which not only has altered all the parameters of numerical calculation but, through miniaturization, has widely diffused large-scale capacity for information processing, storage, and retrieval.

These two basic innovations combine in a variety of ways with four additional developments in communications to produce the hardware of a supposed communications revolution. As they have been widely discussed in the popular press, I will treat them briefly.

First, cable television has radically expanded channel availability and, therefore, the variety of television services available and the capacity to segment the television audience. Cable is practically as old as television for it was first used to import broadcast signals into remote areas or places where topography created signal disturbance. Its contemporary significance is tied to the expansion of channel capacity on the cable and the linkage of cable to an effective means of long distance signalling, namely satellite. In the United States cable has now penetrated 20 percent of television homes and 50 percent of the available markets. While it has not as yet made significant inroads into major cities, it appears to have reached a stage of self-sustaining growth and its potential is enhanced, rather than diminished, by the current inflation and weakness of the economy.

The second development is tele-text, originally a creation of the British Broadcasting Corporation. Tele-text is a process whereby textual material, translated into digital coded data, is inserted into some of the normally unused lines of the television screen. The originating signal can be carried over the air, by telephone or by cable. A decoder built into or added to the television set translates the signal into text and primitive illustrations. The technique has largely been used up to the present for standard, unspectacular fare: news, sports and weather continuously updated; plane and train schedules, classified advertising, yellow pages, etc. The tele-text process is essentially an electronic book. The "pages" turn in fixed succession and at a fixed, and boringly slow, pace. The British Post Office developed an interactive process with the generic name "vu-data" in which the viewer is able to call out what he or she wants. This process requires, naturally, a telephone or cable hook-up. Certainly the most novel feature of the vu-data system is the ability to call in a message to a home television set and to leave it stored there for subsequent retrieval.

Tele-text and vu-data have experienced the most sophisticated development in Europe. However, CBS has been testing a system in Salt Lake City and St. Louis; the Knight Ridder papers are experimenting with a system in Florida and there are a variety of local attempts to test the technical and, above all, commercial feasibility of such systems around the United States.

The third development is that of home disc receivers for

direct satellite to home reception. Such receivers were predicted by Arthur C. Clarke in 1947 and this past winter were available as a Neiman-Marcus special for $36,000. However, the price of the receivers is falling dramatically—an adequate one is now available for $10,000—and while they are not likely to become as cheap as some enthusiasts predict, it is likely that one will be available for around $2,000.

The fourth and final development is home recording devices for which "Beta-max" has become an almost generic name. Such devices break the temporal lock step of viewing and along with a related innovation, video discs, can turn television into a visual-phono record industry. When a simple computer is "interfaced" between a television screen and a video disc "turntable" one can reconstruct and rearrange visual experience, turn video tape into a sequence of photographic slides and rearrange the order and pacing of the visual experience.

The growth of satellite broadcasting and computing capacity along with the four ancillary developments I have noted has created a struggle for the reorganization and control of the communications industry in the United States. We are in a period that corresponds to the early years of movies and radio when armed struggle between various commercial groups representing diverse interests—equipment manufacturers, existing entertainment enterprises such as theatre owners and vaudeville companies, upstart groups such as garment makers—competed to shape and dominate the new media. as with previous media, the intensity of competition is likely to last at least a decade at which time a settled and agreed pattern will emerge. However, this time around, as with every turn of the technological screw, the capital costs will be much greater. IBM, Xerox, and Connecticut General Insurance have formed a consortium for the long distance transmission of business data. The Bell system is now faced with unprecedented competition in its traditional markets and, therefore, begins to penetrate new markets for information and entertainment. On this side of the market it encounters newspapers, cable companies, and a host of new firms trying to organize "home communication systems." The networks resist the incursion of cable and simultaneously hedge their bets by buying into cable companies. Local cable franchisees generally include a small number of local investors—usually as a necessary means of securing the franchise—with the majority stock held by national firms such as American Television and Communications. That firm is owned in turn by Time-Life Inc., which also owns Home Box Office, one of the principal offerings of the cable systems and controls, as well, the distribution rights for B.B.C. programming in America.

There will be a protracted struggle among all these groups to determine how the new services will be divided, integrated, organized, and controlled. The kinds of services we receive from this new technology, and how we pay for it, will be decisively affected by just which groups come to dominate the industry. The fact that radio was first organized by equipment interests and film by entertainment interests is part of the explanation for the differences between those media. So, the struggle will not merely be for profits and control but also for the determination of content and the ways in which the audience will be partitioned and united.

While earlier struggles over the control of new media have largely taken place in a domestic or national context, the present struggle has significant international dimensions. The division of the international broadcasting spectrum, the control of satellite space, the availability of direct satellite to home reception across national boundaries, the deliberate importation of foreign signals, the progressive regional integration of international broadcasting networks—all these issues are on the agenda of the United Nations and subsidiary organizations and in a dozen international boards, tribunals, and conferences. The military, political, and commercial stakes in this contest will shape international relations into the next century.

The most visible evidence that this destabilization has effected the international community is seen in the United Nations. For the past decade UNESCO has been staging conferences, projects, and studies on the role of communication in modern life, particularly in the life of developing nations. Many of these conferences center on the predictable themes of the inequalities of international news flow and on the demand for a "New World Information Order." What developing nations correctly sense is that the new technology of communication has the potential for further centralization of the control of information and the possibility that older forms of colonialism would persevere in new modes of cultural imperialism exercised through the mass media.

Western nations and Western journalists understandably sense in the call for a new information order an erosion of traditional Western beliefs in freedom of information and the justification of censorship of the flow of international news. This conflict gave rise to the MacBride Commission and its study of the totality of human communication. The final report of the commission, a report which is not likely to lessen international conflict in this area, . . . [was] presented to the 21st UNESCO General Conference in Belgrade in the fall of 1980.

Aspects of this same debate have erupted in the United Nations Committee for the Peaceful Uses of Outer Space which has concerned itself with space law, the exploration of outer space, and the use of direct broadcast satellites and remote sensing devices; at the World Administrative Radio Conference that met in Geneva in the fall of 1979; and at the United Nations Conference on Science and Technology for Development in Vienna in 1978.

The official American position on questions of international communication has hardened in response to the United Nations debates and the demands of developing countries. The American commission that provided advice to the MacBride Commission reaffirmed basic American values and interests in these matters: freedom to seek, impart, and receive information and ideas as guaranteed in the Universal Declaration of Human Rights, aversion to centralized control, whether by government or the private sector, opposition to censorship and other forms of state control, dedication both at home and abroad to the right of access of journalists to

sources of information, encouragement of standards of profes-
sionalism that paralleled those of American news gatherers,
and advocacy of the free flow of information. The official position of the United States government also has supported the
direct satellite to home reception of television signals across
international boundaries, a position that has been opposed by
a majority of second and third world nations.

In short, the domestic conflict engendered by the recent
explosion of innovation in communications technology will
be experienced with equal or greater intensity in the international arena at least for the balance of this century.

But how can one understand the possible consequences of
this new generation of technology for international communication? One way is to draw an historical parallel between
certain developments in communication in the United States
in the 19th century and what is occurring in the international
arena today. In short, the history of American experience may
be some guide to contemporary developments. There is, I am
quick to assert, nothing privileged or exceptional in American
experience. However, there is a germ of truth in the title of
Jeremy Tunstall's book of a few years back, *The Media Are
American.* Tunstall did not merely mean that the United
States is the major exporter of news and entertainment,
though he did mean that. Nor did he merely mean that
American media set well nigh universal formats for the
media—length of a feature film, the organization of a news
magazine, the generic types of television content—though he
meant that. Tunstall's title principally refers to the fact that
the mass media penetrated the social fabric more quickly and
deeply in the United States than other countries. By 1835
Alexis de Tocqueville observed that the press in the United
States was second only to public opinion as a force in social
life. By 1850 the United States had become the center of the
cheap daily press, a press which reached deep down into the
habits of manual workers before the European press was
reaching much of the middle class. By this period there were
two hundred daily papers here, more than the rest of the
world combined. With mass communication as with much

else Gertrude Stein's quip is accurate: the United States is really the oldest country in the world for it was first into the twentieth century and has been there the longest. So without making special claims for American experience it nonetheless might provide something of a quick sketch or a shorthand model for likely developments in the international arena in the years immediately ahead.

Between 1835 and the end of the 19th century the basic pattern of social communication in the United States was created, a pattern which exists today in only slightly modified form. The basic technological force in forming this pattern was the telegraph and indeed the telegraph stands to 19th century developments in domestic communication as satellite transmission stands to developments in international communication today. Let me sketch out then, some of the critical developments in communications in the 19th century in the United States in order to engage in some prognostic work concerning the contemporary period. But first, we need some outline, however brief, of the early period of communications in this country.

The American system of communications was established in the late 18th century at a dividing line—what Daniel Boorstin calls a "verge"—in the history of communications. Social communication in that period was organized around established habits of speech and discourse. It was not only that the basic transactions of life were carried on in and mediated by speech—verbal discourse; but that the habits, talents, and opportunities for speaking in public and for speaking to strangers were widespread.

On these habits, customs, conventions of speaking in public were overlaid newer habits of reading, particularly reading what was novel, original, unique, individual, new: news and the newspaper. On the one hand, newspapers were read in public, partly because of limited availability; and, on the other hand, they were read aloud, partly because the habits of private, interiorized reading had not been learned and were not aesthetically satisfying.

The "new" newspaper connected to the oral tradition in a

second way. The content of the newspaper was primarily talk. The newspaper contained speeches, sermons, discourse, public talk: what was being said, discussed, argued in public places. The early American newspaper, then, amplified and extended speech: public opinion or, better, the opinions then being expressed in public. The early newspapers depended then on access to public space: spaces where people gathered to talk and in a developing urban society gathered to talk not solely to intimates but to strangers. The relationship between the newspaper and talk also depended on a group of social habits: the ability to express oneself in public, particularly around strangers, the ability to welcome strangers easily, a reticence to mark those status distinctions which inhibit public talk and discussion. The relationship also depended on the availability of the opinions of others, opinions against which one's own opinions could be formed and, through a dialectic, several opinions could be molded into a consensual one. These conditions give us one of our earliest definitions of a public: a public is a group of strangers who gather to discuss the news. And it gives us also the critical role of certain institutions—public houses—in the ground conditions of the American system of communications.

It was these ground conditions that were protected in the First Amendment safeguards on speech, press, and assembly. Madison's version of the First Amendment which protected freedom of speaking and writing—the activities—makes this clearer than Jefferson's accepted version which places greater emphasis on the institutions. In Madison's version the First Amendment protected speaking and its technical amplification; it protected the public sphere—a zone where private identity could be shed and one could become a public man, a citizen. The originating conditions of American communications required then a public sphere, habits of public discourse, protection of that sphere and discourse from state control, and some means to technically amplify discourse. It is for the protection of those conditions, not simply so that we can find out the price of pork, that the First Amendment assumed importance historically.

Now I've idealized this situation to be sure but only to grasp a sea change that had explicitly crested as a result of a series of technical changes in the 19th century. These changes undercut the ground conditions of communication and did so in two opposing—that is dialectically related—directions. First, technological improvements drove down the cost of the newspaper. This did not necessarily make the newspaper more widely available among literate groups. It merely put the newspaper into everyone's hand and therefore encouraged private reading. The displacement of public reading was a necessary condition for widening the market and it therefore accompanied new patterns of middleclass living emphasizing the private home and the delivery of services—including the newspaper—into such homes. The new habits of private reading led to the deconstitution and reconstitution of the public. First, private reading was tied to the erosion of public space and public habits of speech and discourse. The public, deconstituted into private readers, was now reconstituted as an audience: a group that did not interact with one another but were informed on events of significance as shaped, selected, indeed as constructed by a new professional guild: the journalist as reporter. Private reading cultivated private consciousness of individual members of the audience. Such opinions were not developed for testing in public for the public forum was gone. What was called public opinion was transvalued into the statistical aggregation of private opinions. Discourse became confined to the arena of intimates—relatively safe zones—or in the extreme to imaginary conversation in the heads of audience members: the public was interiorized, psychologized on the basis of private reading. And finally, the press ceased to amplify speech or public discourse; rather it informed its audience, it brought facts, information on which the private audience could forge a judgment.

One dimension of the sea change then was the transformation of publics into audiences and the assemblage of them into larger and larger collectivities, which ingested centralized sources of supply into private zones of reception.

The second dimension of change was the secondary transformation of audiences into groups; the segregation of the assembled audience into national strata. This involved a secondary disruption of the public sphere and of those historic groups which antedated industrialization—regional groups—or were formed during its early migratory phases—ethnic and linguistic groups. The agency of this segregation was the national magazine in significant part but even local newspapers and the wire services contributed through the departmentalization of the press. The growth of the wire services and national transportation allowed for thin national segments to be scored out of the population and unified on the basis of an interest, hobby, vocation, avocation, private opinion. In any given place there were too few of whatever—theosophists, anarchists, fundamentalists, hobbyists, gardeners—but nationally they constituted a valued audience. This segregation forged new but thinned identities, transformed old cultural categories into new media segments—women, children—and everywhere undercut the local and particularistic in favor of the national and segmental. Indeed, the local now became reconstituted by the relations of the segments.

The two-dimensional relationship—the formation of the mass and creation of the segment—represented centripetal and centrifugal forces in the development of modern social structures. One capacity of late 19th century technology assembled and the other capacity disassembled; one aggregated, one segregated. But both tendencies undercut historic identity, the public sphere as a realm of discourse among strangers, a palpable role for citizenship beyond private reading and private opinion, and privatized the very idea of a social relation.

It is important to recognize the role of technology in this. High speed printing so reduced the cost of the newspaper—and subsequently the magazine—that each person could possess the paper as a commodity, could own it and read it as an individual member of an audience. The telegraph allowed the cost of any piece of material to be rationalized over a wider market and thereby encouraged the progressive enlargement of the spatial boundaries of communication.

But to put the matter this starkly is to neutralize the actual historical process that occurred. It was not merely that a national mass audience was formed or that individual taste and interests that were thinly distributed over space were aggregated into the pages of national periodicals. This entire process proceeded on the basis of a particular geographical bias.

The pattern of American communication that developed was the result of competition for control among the major cities of the eastern seaboard. Arthur Schlesinger Sr. described this as a pattern of city state imperialism in which Boston, New York, Philadelphia, and Baltimore reached out to the hinterland to control not only the flow of trade and commerce but also the flow of culture and communication. It is impossible here to go into the details of this competition but what needs to be noted is that by the middle of the 19th century New York dominated the flow of communication throughout the country and other regions existed pretty much as its hinterland. New York newspapers were the models of those in other regions; the wire services were headquartered in New York as were the major magazine and book publishing houses. There were attempts by other cities and regions to develop local traditions of communications and there was considerable regional resentment of New York's dominance. However, the geographical bias to American communication, once set, has continued down to the age of television. The telegraph, in effect, put everyone in the same place for purposes of communication. But the culture and communication that flowed into these places pretty much represented a view of the world and a taste in art and information was dominant in our principal cosmopolitan center.

Once the American system had standardized space so that the same material was available in pretty much the same format independent of where one lived, there developed an attempt to more closely standardize time. Standard time zones, a product of the railroad and telegraph, were established in 1883 to more closely coordinate activity across the nation. The one period reserved from the incursion of commerce, the Sabbath, was progressively invaded in the same decade with the spread of the Sunday newspaper. Newspapers also began multiple editions and started to spread into the evening and early morning. By the mid-20th century 24-hour radio and television stations, 24-hour newspapers would blanket the country—now in both space and time—with mass produced communications. And once this system was established on a domestic basis the United States—and other countries as well—leapt into the international arena. International transmission of radio, international editions of magazines and newspapers, the international distribution of film, the spread of the major wire services represented an attempt to make the international system the arena from which news and culture could be drawn and the market over which the production costs and income potential of mass produced communications could be rationalized.

It is my suggestion that new developments in communications technology have the primary effect of extending and intensifying the pattern and logic of communication so briefly described above. Satellite and cable transmission mean that for purposes of communication everyone in the world is in the same place. Further, with satellites cost disappears as an effective barrier to transmission: in terms of both cost and space everyone is in the same place. As with the early telegraph and newspaper, this creates first of all the potential for a new mass audience, an audience for the private reception of world news, information and culture that in principle includes everyone. The competitors to control the flow of culture and communication in this vastly extended space are not the seaboard cities of America but the major nation states. The media *are* American but they are also British and French and German and Japanese and Russian—and soon others will join the race to control space itself for reasons of political, commercial, and military advantage.

This ability to blanket space will also carry with it the attempt to both coordinate time over larger reaches and to open up time to the incursion of larger amounts of mass produced culture. This ability to control time and space on an international scale will meet with (is being met with) the same regional resistance and reaction that accompanied the growth of a national system of communication in the United States in the 19th century. The current recrudescence of ethnic nationalism is both the reaction and reassertion of historic cultures in the face of the transforming powers of international communication.

Finally, and much more speculatively, I sense as well the growing tendency to select out thin strata of the population across the face of the globe and to unify them into new international segments. One hears this in United Nations rhetoric concerning women and children: single issue groups on a world scale. One hears it as well in the particular versions of speech that are shared by public administrators everywhere, in international congresses of scientists, in the easy movement of professionals among multinational corporations and international bureaucracies. That is, the same pattern of massification and segmentation of the audience that was the achievement domestically of the 19th century now appears, fueled by the ease and flexibility of communication and travel, in international life.

There has developed in recent years a group of metaphors—the "global village," "spaceship earth"—which are designed to bring into consciousness the extraordinary degree of interdependence among the nations and peoples of the earth and the degree to which the spread of the technology of communication on a world scale has brought everyone into awareness of their neighbors in the world. These metaphors themselves recall how this same sentiment was felt on a national scale in the late 19th century. The organic metaphors which characterized transportation and communication—the railroad and the telegraph—as the nervous and arterial system of a national society were aimed at expressing and celebrating the unity of national consciousness and culture that 19th century technology facilitated. In the case of the United States Walt Whitman was the poet laureate of this developing: he heard *America* singing, not its separable states and peoples, over the telegraph and telephone and in the mass newspaper and magazine.

There is reason, of course, to celebrate the potential for international unity and understanding present in new forms of technology, just as the hymns of Whitman caught part of the truth of the 19th century. It is now possible, in principle, to make all the peoples of the world part of the same audience, to have everyone simultaneously aware of matters of common interest and concern. It is possible to bring together smaller groups from around the globe who share a common occupation, avocation, hobby, or interest. And as this bringing together enhances the potential for cooperative work and shared understanding among people otherwise divided by language, tradition, and national boundary, it must be recognized as one of the hopeful developments of our time.

But there is many a slip 'tween the cup and lip, and it is well to be aware of the dangers inherent in this new technical expansion lest we blindly duplicate many of the events of the 19th century that culminated in 1914.

The spread of communication on a world scale has not so much produced common understanding or world brotherhood as it has intensified competition among peoples. The modern competition is not merely among nation states but now among regional blocs of nations—the three worlds, the Eastern vs. the Western nations, the Common Market vs. North America. Far from achieving unity or promoting world government, modern technology raises the scale of the competitive alignments from the state to the region.

Moreover, the new flow of international communication proceeds with its own geographic bias. Rather than an even-handed development of all the world's peoples and cultures it promotes the interests, tastes and concerns of but a few of the world's cosmopolitan centers. On the basis of present evidence there will be years of discord and conflict as peoples who feel themselves squeezed to the margin by these technical developments attempt to maintain and assert a way of life and an historic body of experience in the face of the forces that would eliminate them. Just as the 19th century technology raised national barriers higher as it deregionalized and deracinated its own cultural interiors, so today this process is extended on a world scale and generates predictable response from all those threatened by it. Finally, the new common interest groups that develop on a world scale have the unfortunate potential of extending the class system on a world scale. People come to feel more at home with their peers in other countries that are engaged in common activities, occupations, and avocations than they do with their own countrymen or those in the same geographic community. This spread of international communication inevitably has a class bias (it unites bankers more easily than bookkeepers, managers more easily than manual laborers) and as it facilitates new forms of fellow feeling, it also extirpates older forms of contact and community.

There is perhaps one iron law of communication. Technical advances in this area not only facilitate communication they also depress it; they not only advance mutual understanding they make its widespread achievement more difficult. The printing press spread a common culture on a hitherto unimagined scale, but the printing press also eliminated Latin as a common European language for religion, scholarship, and politics. While it is merely a necessary hypothesis, necessary so that we do not blindly duplicate the "sins of our fathers," it is worth considering that in the arena of international communication, the more things change, the more they remain, on an enlarged scale, the same.

ELECTRONIC DEMOCRACY: HOW TV GOVERNS[1]

ANNE RAWLEY SALDICH[2]

Public lectures are a tradition at Stanford University. It was in the spirit of this tradition that Anne Rawley Saldich was invited to talk about her research for *Electronic Democracy: Television's Impact on the American Political Process* (Praeger, 1979). The timing seemed right. It was a presidential election year and people had become increasingly aware of television's political role in the campaign.

---

[1] Delivered as a public lecture at Stanford University, Palo Alto, California, on February 7, 1980.
[2] For a biographical note, see Appendix.

The idea for a lecture was initiated by Stanford's Director of News and Publications who had read Saldich's book and it was picked up by the Assistant Director for Public Affairs at the Hoover Institution. Ultimately, the Hoover Institution and the Association for Students at Stanford University co-sponsored the talk.

Saldich emphasized that television governs in many subtle ways; that its impact on authority, order, community, and credibility may be invisible and immeasurable but that it is indisputable. She was particularly concerned that journalists and broadcasters have usurped certain governmental functions that are normally the privilege of those elected or appointed to public office, and are not constrained by the usual democratic system of checks and balances.

Although trained as a political scientist, Saldich became interested in the relationship between television and the political process when she started research for her doctoral dissertation at the University of Paris. There, under the direction of Raymond Aron, she analyzed de Gaulle's use of TV as an instrument of power. Since then she has written and lectured on the same theme in the American context. Her current research interests have broadened to include international telecommunications, particularly with respect to video diplomacy.

The speech was delivered to an audience of between 70 and 100 faculty members and interested people from the community in room 2 of the History Corner, Stanford University, Palo Alto, California, at 8 P.M. on February 7, 1980.

Last December when TV's coverage of the mideast crisis was at full flood an Iranian was quoted as saying: "We've got America right by the networks." What he meant was that our hearts and minds soon· would follow. That idea just about sums up two centuries of journalism's growth in the United States: our once-penny sheets are now powerful institutions. Perhaps because it is accepted political practice in his country, the Iranian seems to have understood better than we that television does govern. That is the pivot around which I will develop three problems in electronic democracy: how TV governs, why the First Amendment should apply differently to television than to print, and the need for public accountability.

My context is commercial network news, specifically ABC, CBS, and NBC. Although technological innovations, such as cable and satellite communication, now challenge their leadership it is instructive, nonetheless, to trace how television gradually moved beyond reporting events and influencing the government to functioning as government itself.

By network TV I mean national television. Hundreds of local stations throughout the country choose to affiliate with one of several conventional broadcast networks from which they get much of their programming, including the network's news feed of national and international events. Some stations are independent of networks. They pick and choose their programming from a wide variety of suppliers, but most stations are affiliated with one of the big three.

In deference to the practice of defining one's scope and terms, I would like to say what I mean by "government" and by "sovereignty of the people."

"Government" is used here in two ways: the institutionalized government that we think of on the national, state, and local levels which, in all cases, is divided into three branches: executive, legislative, and judicial. The other definition of "government" is all-encompassing. To use Thomas Jefferson's phrasing, it means the people themselves acting in their political capacity.

The other term that can do with a bit of citation is "sovereignty of the people." I am told by a well-known political scientist who specializes in American government that this country has no sovereign. That may be modern but I have decided it is inaccurate. I believe Alexis de Tocqueville's interpretation of this phrase is still valid. In Part II of his *Democracy in America* he wrote that "above all the institutions, and beyond all the forms, there is a sovereign power, that of the people [because] they can abolish or change them as it will." This classic definition is the one that I use.

Let me begin, now, to crystallize the three points that I make. First, observation shows that television has openly usurped certain functions that are traditionally governmen-

tal. In addition, TV continually shapes our political values
and most of our electoral process in ways that are far from
open.

Second, freedom of the press belongs to the people, not to
journalists. Therefore, it seems to me that the First Amendment should not protect TV in the same way that it protects
print because the airwaves are public property, legally.
Broadcasters would like us to think television news is an extension of print but it is not. It is different, intrinsically and
profoundly.

My last point is that television has a potential for tyranny.
We can guard against it only if TV's vast powers are checked
and balanced through public accountability, just as all political power is checked and balanced wherever democracy is
strong.

Well, in what way does TV govern? The ways are numerous and subtle but four are obvious. Network executives have
taken over what political scientists call gatekeeping, setting
the nation's political agenda, being a court of last resort, and
a conduit for TV diplomacy. Television's bid for a fifth governmental function collapsed when the networks tried to
control the start of TV's presidential campaign last fall.

Gatekeeping is just what it sounds like, control of access
to power. In this context it means control of the airwaves. No
one may appear on national TV without network permission.
That includes presidents. Until recently presidential requests
were quickly met, usually without question. However, after
Nixon and Watergate gave us the journalist-as-hero, network
executives began to flex their political muscle. They have denied access to President Carter on more than one occasion.
An example will suffice. CBS turned down the president's
proposal for a nationwide speech on energy in 1977. The
White House wanted to broadcast "live" but CBS decided
the subject did not warrant interruption of their programming. Since the big three march in lockstep, it surprised no
one when ABC and NBC followed suit. So, for the first time
since his inauguration, Carter formally requested broadcast

time, citing national urgency as his reason. Face was saved on
all sides: he got access and the networks demonstrated independence.

Consider the political implications, even the absurdity of
this situaiton. Who gave network executives this gatekeeping
function? Ours is an electronic democracy, by which I mean
much of the information in our society is transmitted elec-
tronically, and democracy assumes an informed citizenry.
Presidents must have access to the viewing public because
they comprise a majority of the body politic. It is not unusual
for eighty million people to watch a televised presidential address and millions more listen on radio. After all, the public
owns the airwaves and the president is our duly elected representative. No one elected or appointed broadcasters to control presidential access to the nation's electorate or our access
to the president.

Another governmental function that networks exercise
every day is this: on their evening news they set the country's
political agenda, which simply means they pick and choose
what is important for us to know about public affairs. We
have no nationwide, general newspaper in the United States
except for electronic news on radio and television. Of the
two, TV has the greater impact.

Historically it was a nation's leaders, whether religious or
secular, who decided what the people would know about
public affairs. I am not saying that that was a better system.
There was a great deal of deception in the good old days just
as there has been in our recent past and as there may be now.
But that is how government did work and in a democratic society such as ours people could at least vote their leaders out
of office if they thought they were wide of the mark. Today,
however, broadcasters pick and choose what many people
will know and when they will know it. Despite the fact that
TV has a long, well documented track record of not telling us
what we need to know, in order to make intelligent political
choices, broadcasters cannot be voted out of this governmental function. Furthermore, they think that we the people
should have no say about news content. This attitude reflects

a certain arrogance of power. Journalists have forgotten that freedom of the press belongs to the people. It does not belong to a particular profession. Furthermore, the airwaves are public property, legally. They are licensed to stations for three years and are relicensed on condition that the public's interest, convenience, and necessity is ascertained by the station and met. Otherwise the Federal Communications Commission, an arm of Congress, may reassign the license to another station manager. The conclusion is obvious: the public has a right to influence news standards that govern content because they have a right to influence the use of their property.

Because democracy requires an informed citizenry news sources receive special privileges. Print is posted at lower rates than otherwise would apply and broadcasters are awarded monopolies when they are assigned space on the TV spectrum. But TV news is superficial, fragmented, and often irrelevant to the needs of its viewers. Its prime mover is not the public's interest but the public's pocketbook. TV's "half hour" news is twenty-two minutes long. The other eight are sold to advertisers for rates that swing widely between eighty to a hundred and fifty thousand dollars, or more, for every thirty seconds of publicity, depending on how many warm bodies a network delivers to advertisers. X number of viewers are sold for Y number of dollars, like so many bales of hay. Therefore, networks try to build up massive audiences by having something for everyone. The result is that we learn very little about a lot. This has serious consequences for democracy because most Americans use TV as one of their information sources about public affairs and a majority of that group use it as their sole source. That alone is impressive. But TV also enjoys the highest credibility rating of all media, not because the quality of the news is good but because it reaches a national audience and people tend to believe what they see. We often forget that cameras can lie and there are myriad ways to distort reality on television, intentionally or inadvertently. The superficiality of TV news is a disservice to democracy because it is unsuitable as a source of information for participation in the political process. As long as broadcasters control the nation's daily political agenda the public should oblige them to produce quality news that is relevant.

Ironically, it is news coverage which gave network executives another governmental function. TV has become a court of last resort, a corridor to power, for many people who are normally shut out of our political process. When the have-nots decided to have more they took their case to the viewing public. Through massive demonstrations and occasional violence anti-war protestors, blacks, American Indians, women, the aged and infirm dramatized their problems to the nation as a whole and this forced authorities to respond. Street politics became a carefully honed fine art as each group taught others how to manipulate public opinion, via TV, with the same skill and insight as advertisers, government leaders and media managers.

The story of democracy in America parallels closely the development of communications. New technology facilitates the flow of information and allows the underprivileged to see how the other half lives. This has led to an electronic revolution of rising expectations. Although we live in the age of future shock the same maxim is true today that was true in biblical times: knowledge is power. In this context, television's contribution to democracy cannot be overestimated. Ordinary people have used TV to widen and deepen the meaningfulness of America as a land of opportunity for themselves. They have learned that the political process is not limited to an occasional turn at the ballot box. Four years separate one presidential election from another, but TV's combined network news reaches 55 million people night after night during those intervening 208 weeks. Now, that's what you call raw political power.

With regard to television's role as diplomat, the benchmark year was 1977 when Walter Cronkite facilitated an Israeli-Egyptian rapprochement. On a news program that was carried overseas by satellite he helped to arrange an historic visit between the leaders of two nations whose previous relationship had been one of war and bitterness. The most recent sample of TV diplomacy is the Iranian crisis, but that is so familiar it needs no recounting.

Still, it is worth asking: what is the significance of TV diplomacy? In one sense the simple answer is: not much. There's a long history of business serving as a conduit for diplomacy when normal channels of official communication break down. While I wouldn't say that broadcasting is a business like any other (because it has more power than any governmental, economic, or social institution) it is, nonetheless, a multinational corporation with profit motives and business interests that are much the same as Mobil Oil, IBM, or IT&T. Like them, networks have governmental contacts in nations where they station personnel, who are similarly subject to temptations of privilege and corruption. So, in this regard, journalists trod a well worn path when they were chosen as a conduit for information exchange by both governments. (We've heard a great deal about the Iranians manipulating television, but the White House spokesman for the Iranian crisis was Hodding Carter III, whose professional credentials include seventeen years as a reporter and editor. That is not a coincidence.)

The yet undefined significance of TV diplomacy allows one's fantasies to roam. Perhaps modern warfare could be ritualized on TV as global theatre. Why not a war of words? Why not a holocaust of orchestrated street demonstrations any video frenzy? We could have a military draft system that would train an army of camera crews to fight on foreign soil, shooting film instead of missiles. Staging centers could be set up, under allied protection, where other military personnel study intensively for starring roles as tyrants or government negotiators. Instead of the classic infantry we could have a sort of televised Greek chorus, chanting in unison: The whole world's watching! Then, if a Canadian camera crew comes along to film, the chorus could salute or exploit that country's separatist tendencies by switching to French: le monde entier nous regarde!

Ridiculous? Sure. But not more so than many a ridiculous war that is now part of history.

The point is this: television received a lot of instant criticism for filling a function that is normally governmental, even though there is a long tradition of business becoming an information exchange when diplomatic channels break down. Perhaps it would be worthwhile to consider the positive possibilities of international TV as a forum, an electronic United Nations, through which nations could let off steam when the pressure builds up.

Is there a conspiracy among networks to take over the government? I doubt it. Most broadcasters have been slow to understand the nature of their vast political power and few admit they threaten or have taken over certain facets of governing. Television acquired political power gradually, almost imperceptably, without plotting and scheming, as a spillover effect from video technology. However, a recent move by the networks to take on another governmental function did seem to be calculated.

In the fall of last year television executives decided they would not sell half hour time segments to political candidates. They said it was too soon to start TV's presidential campaign. Again, the question arises: should broadcasters control the start of a governmental function of this magnitude? As it happens, they did not succeed because candidate Carter appealed to the FCC and the commission overruled the networks.

The issues surrounding this event are enormously complex. One can sympathize with broadcasters because the fairness rule and equal time provision require them to make air time available to all candidates once one has appeared on television. At first glance it does seem "unwarranted," as the networks put it "to interrupt their regularly scheduled programming" for the campaign. But if we look at that explanation from a different angle it doesn't make any sense. After all, TV programs are designed to be interrupted, by advertisements that are sold at a princely sum. The CBS news magazine, "60 minutes" earns $200,000 per minute of advertising. And specials are really special when it comes to the bottom line. When the Steelers and Rams met in the Rose Bowl this year advertising sold for $476,000 a minute. With twenty-two commercial minutes during that game we're talking about really big money. Therefore, we could reinterpret the networks' position as follows: presidential campaigns do not warrant the interruption of our regularly scheduled profits. Now they may be right. Surely more people would watch the Rose Bowl than a political candidate. But the start of TV's presidential campaign, in an electronic democracy, is a decision about governing America and it is far too important to be left solely to broadcasters. While the excessive length of our campaigns is worthy of debate it is one in which the public should participate since it is the use of public property that is being discussed.

These are the obvious ways that TV governs. There is no time to elaborate on the subtle ways in which TV affects our political values and how it restructures the electoral process. All I can do is mention a few in passing.

Personalizing power is one that comes to mind. Whoever is before the camera's eye gains ground for that episode of Who Governs? During Watergate it was the Congress; in the era of street politics it was the protestors; often it is the president; at the end of last year it seemed to be the Ayatollah. There are a few notable exceptions where TV is impressively destructive (for instance, Ted Kennedy's televised condemnation of the Shah) but these prove the rule rather than weaken it.

Another example of subtle shaping is immediacy. Electronic news is hard and fast. Its negative impact on democracy is that it conditions viewers to want immediate answers. But democracy is a bumbling, stumbling, inefficient form of government. It was designed that way to guard against tyranny. Dictatorships seem to be efficient. When journalists ask questions of a dictator the answers can be given immediately and without qualification because few people need to be consulted. In fact, the answers might be given to journalists before they are asked along with a list of questions from which reporters are not to deviate. But in a democracy the best way to preserve freedom is to have an open exchange of ideas, a public debate on matters of consequence. Democracy therefore takes time, whereas television is intolerant of reasoned discourse. Its emphasis is visual and visceral, not rational.

Officials know this. They often think they will look foolish or uncooperative if they don't answer a question put by a TV journalist and so they almost always do. That quickly but imperceptibly reverses the leadership role, putting the journalist in charge. It also reinforces the viewers' impression that there are immediate answers to all issues, no matter how complex, and if officials don't supply them they are guilty of some misdoing.

This kind of thinking ties in with another hidden governmental power that TV exercises daily. Whenever important public policy is decided for the nation the TV factor is always weighed: how will it play on the home screens? This means that TV personnel participate in the government's decision-making process even when they are not there personally. It's a kind of Orwellian remote control, a sort of grey eminence that subtly shapes policy with an invisible hand.

As for restructuring the electoral process, television coverage has weakened parties and conventions and it has caused campaign costs to skyrocket. It is not simply that politicians buy expensive air time, if stations will sell it to them. It has to do with candidates entering as many primaries as possible, with the hope that they will get TV coverage and therefore win national recognition on the nightly news. Every primary costs money, lots of money. If there were a neck and neck race here in California among Brown, Carter, and Kennedy, the state Democratic headquarters tells me that each candidate might be expected to spend between two and three million dollars. In other states where there's not much of a fight (for example, Georgia would probably go to Carter) the contestants might spend as little as a few hundred thousand dollars or less. As Mary Ellen Leary pointed out, the political significance of this is that candidates spend a large part of their time fundraising instead of dealing with issues. For those candidates who already hold office this getting and spending of money takes time away from their governmental responsibilities. For everyone who makes politics a career it is important to accommodate TV by maintaining a good rapport with its reporters and managers. Again, the Orwellian syndrome: even after an office is won there is always the next election to think about, and this gives television personnel additional leverage in day-to-day government. Although much more could be said on this subject it's time to move on to the First Amendment and why I think it should apply differently to television than to print.

Television's immense political power flows from a combination of several qualities that are not found elsewhere. Its powerful imagery gives viewers a you-are-there feeling, which tends to shut down one's critical, analytical faculties. This, in turn, gives the medium high credibility. People are inclined to believe what they see even if it contradicts their knowledge or experience. Because television news has the highest credibility of all media it also enjoys the kind of authority that every institution in America envies. Credibility is the keystone of all power relationships because belief is the engine of action.

Another unique quality that TV enjoys is its vast audience, which can be compared with radio. While the combined network news reaches 55 million viewers on week nights the space shots, President Kennedy's funeral, the Watergate hearings, and President Nixon's resignation, as well as many other TV specials, were seen by billions throughout the world.

And, television news is received more or less simultaneously, depending on time zones. This is unlike newspapers and magazines whose readers read at their convenience, rather than having their news consumption orchestrated nationally as TV's is. Still another characteristic of television is that it is a continuum and cannot be scanned. Just as the TV set dictates at what time people will get their nightly news so it also dictates that everything must be viewed if one is looking for a particular report.

While radio shares many of these characteristics it does not have the visuals, or the highest credibility, nor does it per-

sonalize power in the same way. The source of TV's impact is
the mix of all these qualities. That is why all of the still photos
in all of the print media did not create the same degree of
furor that TV's coverage of the Iranian hostages did. To cite
one source, *Newsweek* had dramatic color photos of two Iranians carrying garbage in a large American flag, they showed
a black hostage against a wall poster that was covered with
anti-American propaganda, other hostages were photo-
graphed in humiliating positions—on the floor with hands
bound. This kind of picture was not confined to *Newsweek*.
Why, then, was there such an outcry when similar images appeared on the home screen? It is because of the medium's
unique combination of qualities which are also its source of
potential for tyranny: immediacy, moving pictures, a vast audience, and more or less simultaneous reception. The impact
has a terrific effect that strains a democratic process because
viewers want instant solutions. But international diplomacy is
a ritual that takes time.

Freedom of the press is a great tradition in America, and
ours has been a model for many countries. Journalists are
quick to defend themselves against tendencies to abridge that
freedom and they are right to do so. However, the press controls most information sources in the U.S. but media managers
seldom admit that they have unmatched political power for
that very reason. Others may spend as much time, money, and
talent in advancing their interests but no institution has the
media's power to investigate for publication, and do so with
social approval. Even the FBI, CIA, and the police need
media cooperation in order to round off their investigations
with publicity. Big business may influence policy at home and
abroad, as do the multinational broadcasting networks, but
they cannot tell their story to the American people unless the
press will sell or give them space and time. Similarly, television executives almost never allow their network or station
problems to be aired and in this way the public is cleverly
manipulated.

Let's consider the case of free TV. Americans who visit
Western Europe are often surprised to learn that an annual

tax is paid on each television set. For color it is about $50 a year and for black and white it is about $35. Figures vary from country to country and are subject to change. Everything about this is fairly straightforward but American tourists are almost always shocked and they usually tell their European friends: Why in our country we have free TV. But that isn't true. We pay a hidden TV tax, because prices of all TV-advertised products are raised a few cents so that we may have the pleasure of viewing commercials. It's a simple little system. Broadcasters use our airwaves at no cost to themselves. Consumers (not just people who own television sets) pay for them to have this opportunity. Manufacturers use our airwaves at no cost, also, because they have passed the advertising bill on, and it is from that fortune in advertising revenue that broadcasters make their enormous profits, enough to pay Barbara Walters a million a year, and to budget eighty thousand dollars annually so that Charlie's angels will have their hair nicely combed when you watch that program. In short, what we have in America is an undeclared system of pay-TV, or, in political terms, of taxation without representation. Why don't most Americans realize this? Because broadcasters have carefully controlled that information. For the same reasons the networks don't like to have themselves discussed as multinational big business. But they are. Nor will their managers readily admit to having governmental power. But they do. And certainly journalists are unlikely to tell us that their role as guardians of the public interest is a self-appointed one. But it is. The First Amendment on which they base their claim also protects religion. Using the same logic that the press has used, there is no reason why legitimate religious leaders and their less respectable counterparts should not appoint themselves as the public's watch dog.

The First Amendment is a part of the Bill of Rights that was written for the people, not for the press. Its wording is clear and simple: "Congress shall make no law abridging the freedom of speech, or of the press . . ." Note, there is no mention of this nation's sovereign, the people. If the First Amendment is not taken out of context, if we keep in mind that the overall purpose of the Constitution is to separate and divide power so that it cannot become tyrannous, then simplicity gives way to complexity. Then, a strong argument can be made that television has staggering political power which should be checked and balanced. Naturally, this interpretation of the Constitution is not the broadcasters' favorite.

Tyranny is the arbitrary use of power in the absence of accountability. This describes television before 1968, which is when Paul Simpson founded this nation's first television news archive for public use. Speaking politically, what he did was to provide us with the means of checking TV's tyrannous potential by documenting how its power is used and making it accountable to the public.

To set the tone for this last theme on accountability I would like to quote Freeman Dyson, an eminent physicist, from his new book, which is titled *Disturbing the Universe:* What he says is this: "Through science and technology, evil is organized bureaucratically so that no individual is responsible for what happens." Think of that in connection with television. A dozen years ago, when there were no TV archives, broadcasters were fond of saying their medium is merely a neutral conduit of information, that their reporters are objective, without bias, that TV is simply a window on the world. What they did not tell us is that what we see depends on where they put the window. Objectivity does not exist but it is a wonderful thing if we can convince others that it does because that frees us from responsibility.

Usually when we think about making TV accountable to the public the first thing that comes to mind is regulation through institutionalized government, such as the FCC. That is not what I advocate. The public accountability that I am thinking of would find expression in press councils, classroom instruction in electronic literacy so that we learn how to watch and listen to television with a new awareness; I would like television archives to expand and proliferate and I would like to see citizens' groups influence standards for news content. That last one is bound to raise the ire of broadcasters for they have accustomed themselves to think that freedom of the press means freedom to do what they please, even though we the people pay them to use our property for their profit. It is a favorite axiom in business that "there ain't no free lunch." I think it is time to let the wealthy multinational networks pick up the tab for some part of this accountability process. Unlike most other businesses they have never had a year without profit since 1940. Wall Street analysts tell us that NBC had a bad year in 1978 when its pre-tax profits bottomed out at $122 million. In the language of transactional analysis that would come under the game called: "Ain't it awful?" We should all have such a bad year.

Teaching electronic literacy should be done in the schools and over the air. Everyone should learn about the absence of truth in advertising, when it occurs, and how to recognize it. We should know how TV shapes values and what the mechanics are for distorting reality. For instance, when blacks rioted in Watts, California, during the sixties TV did not have the fast film that they now have, which allows crews to shoot in the dimmest of light. So, to accommodate the technology that was then available TV photographers, filming at night, sought out available light sources, most of which were fires set by arsonists. Without intending to they distorted reality because the televised version of Watts gave the impression of an entire city aflame, which was not the case, though it did provide good visuals. Electronic literacy would also teach us to find out the source of video materials. Much of the TV film that we saw during the early years of our war in Indochina came from the government in the form of "handouts" which were used by broadcasters without telling us that we were viewing propaganda instead of reports filmed by TV journalists. If Watergate gave us the journalist as hero those early years of fighting in Southeast Asia gave us the journalist-as-dupe. We should all learn how TV technicians can splice together bits and pieces of what a person says so that it bears no resemblance to the actual event. Some astute interviewees prevent this by insisting that they be taped to time, which means that if they grant a ten minute interview the broadcasters must agree to air all ten minutes of it. Or, they might refuse an interview altogether unless it is broadcast "live," thereby circumventing the lab where so much of reality ends up on the cutting room floor. We should also learn to see what is not on our TV screens. Broadcasters keep telling us that TV mirrors society. Really? Where are the American Indians? Where are the Mexican Americans? The Puerto-Ricans? Where and when do we see on our home screens images of intelligent, capable, hardworking people with physical infirmities? Where are the analyses of media's influence on every facet of our lives?

In addition to press councils and electronic literacy much can be done on behalf of public accountability by encouraging interest groups to form media evaluation centers. This has already been done with success by Action for Children's Television and by the United Church of Christ which is to television what Nadar's Raiders are to car manufacturers. Many other organizations have also been effective media activists but TV managers don't like people to know what a lot of power we have. For example, in the spring of 1978 the Parent Teachers Association met in Chicago with nearly twenty executives whose products are advertised on children's programs. The PTA had a simple message: use your influence to get sex and violence off of children's programs or we will lead a nationwide boycott of your products and we have the clout to get others, such as churches and medical institutions, to join us. Their threat was successful. This was a giant step for grass roots democracy. It was an extraordinary coming together of issues and events but network news gave it the silent treatment. They invoked that principle of journalistic folklore that says: if it wasn't reported it didn't happen.

The fourth expression of public accountability is television archives and all the others are really based on their existence, but most particularly on adequate access to their resources.

It was while doing research here at the Hoover Institution that I began to appreciate how important TV archives are to the vitality of electronic democracy. They are as important as the public library system was in the linear era when most information came through print. When I was doing that research I wanted to analyze how each network had reported the American Indians' takeover of Wounded Knee as a protest against injustice. I was able to do this efficiently, at minimal cost, because there is an excellent television news archive at Vanderbilt University in Nashville, Tennessee, which was started by a private citizen with his own funds in 1968. This is not the place to tell you the story of that remarkable institution and how CBS tried to put it out of business. What you want to know is that it exists, that it is service oriented, and that its materials are accessible because that TV archive has troubled itself to put out an index and abstract of its resources that is comparable in comprehensiveness and quality to the New York *Times Index*. Both the Hoover and the Green libraries have these, here at Stanford. To get videotapes from Vanderbilt you simply go through their indices, select news segments that you want to see, list your selections (which are really a reflection of your editorial judgment), and mail it off to Nashville. You will pay a modest user fee, a refundable deposit for the tapes, and you will sign a promise that you will not have public showings of the materials except under certain conditions. In Tennessee the archive technicians will splice together the selections that have been made and in short order you will receive a compiled video subject tape that can be studied with ease. Or, you can request an entire evening's broadcast, as well as certain documentaries and public affairs programs.

There are few video archives in America. The Vanderbilt Television News Archive is the only one that sends materials from its institution to the user, so that research can be done wherever a playback facility exists, whether in libraries, business offices or homes. This gives the researchers considerable flexibility because they do not have to conform to an institution's business hours. Here at Stanford playback machines are available in the Communications library, at the Hoover, in the Education department and probably in several other places of which I have no knowledge.

It is important to know that Vanderbilt's is the only archive that will compile a subject tape for you. The other major video archive is our National Archives in Washington, D.C.

Unwisely, they have let CBS dictate the terms of government policy with respect to their collection and how it is used. CBS, whose whole empire turns on the ability to sell, simply sold the director of the National Archives a bill of goods that prevents the archives from compiling subject matter tapes or sending tapes directly to users. Materials are mailed only from one institution to another. If your library in northwestern Alaska does not have a playback machine, too bad. Try Seattle. In return for letting CBS dictate its policy, the National Archives gets CBS news free of charge and CBS has issued nationwide press releases to advertise its generous gift to the nation.

The political issues involved here are essentially these: CBS is making government policy which denies public access to public events that were broadcast over public property from which activity CBS accrued considerable revenue. Let me give you an example of what I mean by denying access. When I did my research on Wounded Knee it took me three hours to run through those segments of the networks' news coverage that I had asked the Vanderbilt Television News Archive to splice together. Had Vanderbilt signed one of CBS' agreements about the use of video tapes I would have had to request 9 weeks of evening news for each of the networks. That's a total of 135 video cassettes. Imagine retrieving all that from the shelves, packaging it up, mailing it out, being handled by me. Think of the expense in terms of retrieval time and postage. Think of how long I would tie up a playback machine in order to get to one 45 seconds or three minute news segment. Think of how awkward and cumbersome that makes the mechanics of doing research. This is what Dyson means when he says that evil is organized bureaucratically through science and technology.

At this point you are not surprised to learn that NBC and ABC have followed CBS' policies in lemming-like fashion. What the networks are doing is not unlike techniques that were used to keep blacks from voting in the South. This is the broadcasters' version of the poll tax and unreasonable literacy laws. It denies access while appearing to be in the public's interest.

Researchers and educators who understand the importance of television archives should take the lead in petitioning Congress to change our National Archives' policy so that big business (the networks) do not dictate access to public resources. And we should take the lead in working out a system whereby the networks help to support and multiply archives. They can well afford to do this from their profits, as part of their legal commitment to the public interest. There is not much point in knowing about all this unless someone takes action, and I think that burden falls on scholars who understand how documentation is related to accountability, and how accountability is related to freedom.

In closing I want to say again that television has been a great asset to democracy. Sure, there are problems but there are problems everywhere: in education, religion, government, business, and volunteer associations. Broadcasters have not cornered the market on imperfection. The medium is no longer in its infancy but it, and we, are on the learning curve. While we must have the courage to study its political power and governing functions with care, we should do this with the intention of building on its strengths in such a way that future communications technology will continue to protect not only freedom of the press but the people for whom that press is free.

ECONOMIC CHANGE IN THE FUTURE

MEETING THE JAPANESE ECONOMIC CHALLENGE[1]

WILLIAM S. ANDERSON[2]

A major concern of Americans in 1980–1981 was the state of
the economy—spiralling inflation, high unemployment, declining
productivity, and the increasing inability of a growing number of
American industries to compete with their foreign counterparts.
The expanding number of Americans choosing Datsun, Toyota,
and Sony instead of Ford, Chevrolet, and Zenith, and the success
of the Japanese auto makers is serving as a lesson for the West.

William S. Anderson, Chairman of the NCR Corporation, explored the challenge of Japanese economic competition in a
speech at the University of Notre Dame in South Bend, Indiana,
on September 25, 1980. The address, one in the series of ITT Key
Issues Lectures, was presented to an audience made up of 300 to
400 students and faculty members of Notre Dame and St. Mary's
College, local businessmen, and the general public. The lecture,
delivered at 3:30 P.M. in the auditorium of the Memorial Library,
was an excellent example of how a speech in a small locality can
gain national and international attention. Several magazines in the
United States and Japan subsequently published condensed versions of the address while others quoted excerpts from it.

Anderson was well-qualified to discuss the topic, for he was
born, raised, and educated in the Orient, and he spent more than
35 years as a business executive in the Far East. Rising from
his positions as vice-president and chairman of National Cash Register in Japan he was named corporate president, director, and
since 1976, Chairman of the Board of NCR Corporation in this
country.

Anderson centered his speech on the seriousness of the economic challenge for which there is no easy answer. "At stake," he
contended, "is the industrial supremacy which this country has

---

[1] Delivered as one of the ITT Key Issues Lectures in the auditorium of the Memorial
Library of the University of Notre Dame, South Bend, Indiana, at 3:30 P.M. on September
25, 1980.
[2] For biographical note, see Appendix.

enjoyed for most of this century. And it is Japan, more than any
other nation, which exemplifies the seriousness of the challenge to
American industrial leadership." He described Japan's remarkable
economic recovery following World War II and then previewed
his discussion topics with several rhetorical questions:

> Why have the Japanese been so successful? How did the
> United States lose its competitive edge? Can it be regained
> and, if so, how? And will the Japanese economic juggernaut be
> as awesome in the 1980s as it has been in the decade just
> ended? These are the basic questions I should like to explore
> with you.

Anderson organized his speech according to the problem-
solution method. His discussion of the problem—the Japanese
challenge—was almost entirely informational and brought out
his greatest strength: the speaker, because of his background, was
regarded as an authority on the subject.

When I was invited by Dean Furuhashi to lecture on the
subject of "Meeting the Japanese Economic Challenge," I
was both pleased and apprehensive. To participate in this
distinguished lecture series is an honor I deeply appreciate.
On the other hand, I am well aware that the economic challenge facing America today is not a subject for which there
are any easy answers.

Arnold Toynbee once described the rise and fall of nations
in terms of challenge and response. A young nation, he said, is
confronted with a challenge for which it finds a successful response. It then grows and prospers. But as time passes, the
nature of the challenge changes. And if a nation continues to
make the same, once-successful response to the new challenge, it inevitably suffers a decline and eventual failure.

As we begin the last two decades of the 20th century, the
United States faces such a challenge. At stake is the industrial
supremacy which this country has enjoyed for most of this
century. And it is Japan, more than any other nation, which
exemplifies the seriousness of the challenge to American industrial leadership.

Thirty-five years ago, as a witness at the war crime trials

in Tokyo, I saw Japan at the low point of its long history. Its economy was shattered, its political and social fabric torn, and its people demoralized. Those of us who were in Japan immediately after World War II had serious doubts as to whether the nation would ever be a first-rate power.

What has happened since then continues to astonish the world. In a little over three decades, Japan has become the most competitive nation on earth. It has not only caught up with the much better endowed industrial nations of the West; it has in many fields surpassed them. And it has done so by meeting the challenge of a lost war with fresh new responses.

Why have the Japanese been so successful? How did the United States lose its competitive edge? Can it be regained and, if so, how? And will the Japanese economic juggernaut be as awesome in the 1980s as it has been in the decade just ended?

These are the basic questions I should like to explore with you today.

In recent months the media have been flooded with attempts to explain the Japanese phenomenon. Everyone wants to know how the Japanese did it. There are, of course, scores of explanations. But it seems to me that Japan's post-war economic growth—the most spectacular the world has ever seen—is the direct result of two fundamental characteristics of the Japanese nation in the years following World War II.

The first of these is Japan's unerring sense of national purpose and its establishment of clearcut, readily understandable goals reinforced by a willingness to do what was necessary to achieve those goals.

I believe the second major ingredient in the Japanese success forumla is the personality of the Japanese people themselves.

If we are to analyze the Japanese accomplishment, and learn some lessons from that accomplishment, then we must begin with an examination of those two factors.

Just as every American understands that the United States

is rich in natural resources, so every Japanese understands that Japan is one of the poorest endowed countries in the world. It is a country in which 115 million people are squeezed into an area only four times the size of the state of Indiana. It is a country which is almost totally dependent on other countries for oil, coal, iron ore, and most other natural resources. Japan can't even feed itself. Only about 15 percent of its land is suitable for agriculture, and therefore a third of its food supply must come from other nations.

Japan's attempt to enlarge its meager share of the world's resources through military aggression ended disastrously in 1945. Then, in one of the most abrupt turnabouts in all history, the Japanese people reversed direction. In essence, they said this:

In physical resources we are poor, and that will not change. But in human resources we are rich. Our challenge therefore, as a nation and as individuals, is to more fully utilize our human resources than any other country. We will import the raw materials we lack, and through hard work and imagination convert those basic materials into useful products—not only for the Japanese people but for international markets as well.

It was a "you and me against the world" kind of attitude. And the first step in translating that national consensus into an action program was to develop a unique new leadership structure—a structure in which government, business, and labor would form the powerful triumvirate which the world has since labeled Japan, Inc., not in a derogatory sense, as many Japanese fear, but with a sense of envy.

The structure on which Japan, Inc., was built was beautifully simple. In the government sector, the Ministry of International Trade and Industry would develop and promote a national industrial plan. And the Bank of Japan and the Ministry of Finance would supply the capital and carefully control the purse strings in order to keep the new industrial plan on track.

Meanwhile, the doers—that is, business and labor—would be given a relatively free hand to utilize the inherent strengths of the capitalistic system. Taxation and government intervention would be kept to a minimum. Social programs would be deferred until Japan could afford them. Emphasis was to be on the future, not the past, or even the present.

In looking to that future, Japan's vision was clear. Modernization of its industry was given top priority. This required the importation of Western technology as rapidly as possible. The director of the Japan Economic Research Center, Nobuyoshi Namiki, recently gave credit where credit was due, and I quote:

We were quick to learn from the West—especially from the Americans. We were playing the game of catch-up, with a vengeance.

Other nations have also tried to play the catch-up game, but with conspicuous lack of success. Those nations also had a sense of national purpose and readily understandable goals. What made the Japanese different? To answer that question, I believe we have to look to the Japanese character and personality.

According to the American Declaration of Independence, all men are endowed by the Creator with certain unalienable rights, among which are life, liberty, and the pursuit of happiness. If the Japanese were to rewrite that venerable document, I suspect they would amend it to read "life, liberty, and the pursuit of happiness and knowledge."

I hope you'll forgive me for quoting a Harvard professor here on the Notre Dame campus, but I believe that Dr. Ezra Vogel has summed up the intellectual curiosity of the Japanese as well as anyone could. This is what he says:

In virtually every important Japanese organization and community—from the national government to individual private firms, from cities to villages—devoted leaders worry about the future of their organizations. And to those leaders nothing is more important than the information and knowledge that the organizations might one day need. It is not always clear why knowledge is needed, but groups store up available information nonetheless, on the chance that some day it might be useful. . . . In Japan, study is a social activity which continues through life.

This nationwide zeal for learning exhibits itself in countless ways. Millions of Japanese are fluent not only in English but even in third and fourth languages; how many Americans or Britishers speak Japanese? Japan, with half the population of the United States, graduates almost twice as many engineers; that's a per-capita ratio of four to one. And in international testing programs, Japanese youth run rings around their American or British counterparts, not only in math and science subjects but in many other subjects as well. It's no exaggeration to say that Japan is today the most literate, best educated nation in the world.

The second most striking characteristic of the Japanese people is their unquenchable team spirit. Nowhere is this more evident than in the relationship between management and labor.

Many years ago the chairman of General Motors Corporation created a furor by remarking that "What is good for America is good for General Motors and what is good for General Motors is good for America." If the chairman of Toyota were to make a similar remark in Japan today, I doubt if anyone would lift an eyebrow. In Japan, employees are as interested in the growth of their companies, and in the progress of the national economy, as they are in improving their own wages and benefits. They realize it is company growth and national economic growth which have made possible their own rapidly rising living standards.

I do not suggest that Japanese labor unions are weak or their members docile. To the contrary. A higher proportion of workers are unionized in Japan than in the United States. Workers are highly militant. I have had the harrowing experience of sitting in a car at the blocked entrance to NCR's factory in Oiso, surrounded by hundreds of unhapy employees who—to make sure I understood their displeasure—violently rocked the car from side to side before finally permitting me to enter the plant.

Yet long strikes are rare in Japan. In fact, the production time lost because of strikes is only about one-eighth of the days lost in the United States. The reason is that the vast majority of Japanese workers have learned that the team concept works as well on the production line as it does on the athletic field. Whilst they're perfectly willing to squeeze the goose that lays the golden eggs, during every spring labor "offensive," they are very careful not to strangle it to death.

The Japanese are also a proud people, and I use that term in its best sense. As you know, "face" is terribly important to most Orientals, especially the Japanese. World War II ended in international humiliation for Japan. Whether consciously or subconsciously, the Japanese people were determined to make Japan respectable again. What better way to do so than to achieve excellence in everything they undertook? In an economic sense, this translated into no more shoddy merchandise, whose only merit was a lower price tag. Instead, the Japanese vowed to make better cameras than the Germans, better watches than the Swiss, and better radio and television sets than the Americans.

Quality became a national obsession because every Japanese recognized that quality products would not only bring the top dollar required for sustained economic growth but at the same time would restore their country's prestige among nations. And in only a few years, the label "Made in Japan" became the symbol of excellence in a long list of goods—ranging from heavy industrial equipment to everyday consumer products.

Quality in itself, of course, is meaningless if it's lavished on products which no one wants. The Japanese were quick to recognize this. Indeed, their ability to define what the market will buy is probably unequalled by any other country.

This is no accident. The Japanese research a potential market to an almost unbelievable extent. They listen carefully to what the consumer is saying. Then they give him the kind of product he wants, not the kind of product they think he should want. The focus is also on providing greater value to the customer. As a result, Japanese products tend to be better featured than many of their counterparts manufactured in Western Europe or the United States.

Japanese companies also search relentlessly for new applications for older products. No opportunity is too small or remote to be explored. Let me cite a single example:

If you've had occasion to use one of the instant-bonding

"super" glues—the kind that will glue your fingers together if you're not careful—the chances are it came from Japan. The Japanese took a 25-year-old product, originally developed in America for industrial use, repackaged it, and created a new, 100-million-dollar consumer market.

Creating new markets, or penetrating someone else's existing markets, requires patience. This the Japanese have in abundance. One of the characteristics which most distinguish top Japanese management is the emphasis they place on thinking long term rather than short term. On the occasion of his retirement, the founder of Honda Motor Company, Soichiro Honda, was able to say, and I quote:

The deputy president and I have not signed any papers nor attended any executive committee meetings for the past 10 years. We have done what presidents should do; we have spent our time correctly judging future trends. That is our job. The details of day-to-day operation we leave to the responsible personnel.

This is in sharp contrast with the operating style of most American and European business managers. In the West, long-term corporate strategy tends to play second fiddle to short-term performance. The shareholder owners of the company want results now, not five or 10 years from now. And the management that fails to report consistent progress from quarter to quarter quickly falls out of favor with the investment community. The result is a strong temptation to avoid costly investment in basic research and to shy away from new markets which over the short term would only detract from profitability.

This is not to say that the typical Japanese manager is disinterested in short-term results; to the contrary, the Japanese businessmen I've dealt with are just as closely oriented to the profit-and-loss statement as their Western counterparts. The difference is that the Japanese business manager is less likely to lose sight of what his company could be doing five or 10 years out, provided the proper investment for that future is made today.

In this attitude he is in close harmony with the average Japanese, who is also strongly future oriented—in contrast with the "now" attitude so prevalent today in Western countries.

The typical Japanese household sets aside 20 percent of its total income for a rainy day. That is the highest rate of personal savings of any country. It compares with a personal savings rate of less than 5 percent in the United States, which is the lowest of any developed nation. This, of course, helps explain why gross capital formation in Japan is approximately the same as in the United States, even though the U.S. economy is twice as large as the Japanese economy.

When one economic system is generating twice as much per-capita funds for investment as another economy, all kinds of favorable things begin to happen. New industries can be started and old industries brought up to date. And Japanese tax laws actively encourage an already thrifty people to become even more so.

The actual figures on industrial investment are sobering. During the past year Japan's investment in new plant and equipment has totaled 17 percent of Gross National Product. That compares with only 7.5 percent here in the United States.

But perhaps the greatest catalyst for Japan's remarkable economic achievements has been its near-obsession with finding new ways to increase personal and group productivity. Indeed, the Japanese people come very close to worshiping productivity. We see this in virtually every industry in which they have chosen to compete. The most dramatic recent example is the phenomenal growth of the Japanese auto industry. Twenty years ago Japan produced fewer than 100,-000 automobiles a year. Today the Japanese auto industry has accelerated past the European auto industry and is now on the verge of overtaking America's auto industry as well.

In automobiles—as in steelmaking, camera production, or almost any other Japanese manufacturing operation—productivity is nothing short of amazing. The latest study I've seen shows that Toyota is producing 50 cars per man year compared with fewer than 20 cars per man year for any European manufacturer.

How have they done it? That's what the president of the

Ford Motor Company wanted to find out. So he sent whole teams of people to study this latest Japanese miracle. They reported that it's largely a matter of productivity-oriented methods and management, plus an unusually high degree of automation.

At Toyo Kogyo, where Mazda cars are manufactured, there are only five organizational levels between the production-line employee and the vice president in charge of manufacturing. This compares with a dozen layers of management in a typical European or American auto company.

The Ford study teams also found that the Japanese workers maintain their production equipment so carefully that machine breakdowns almost never occur. As a result, Toyo Kogyo can get by with carrying only one or two hours' supply of parts inventories to keep their production lines running. This compares with parts inventories for as much as three weeks in the plants of their American and European competitors.

In addition, suppliers are closely keyed into the production system. The supplier of ornamental trim, for example, drives his loaded truck right into the assembly plant and personally unloads it at the production line. Then he picks up the empty containers, puts them back on his truck, and—believe it or not—actually tidies up the area before returning to his own plant for more parts.

This clocklike approach drastically reduces factory space requirements. It lowers overhead and material-handling costs and reduces the number of employees required to turn out a given number of cars. To quote the president of Ford Motor Company, where the concept of the production line was born:

All the Japanese have really done is to take Henry Ford's basic principle—that is, keep the production line moving in a continuous, rhythmic, dedicated process—and go a few, admittedly brilliant steps further.

Innovative use of supplier capabilities is widespread in Japanese industry. Nippon Steel, with half as many employees as U.S. Steel, achieves approximately the same output.

Part of this is due to Nippon's more modern plant, but the biggest factor is that the Japanese steel company makes extensive use of low-wage subcontractors. This holds down their own labor costs and results in more steel per dollar of wages.

In many industries, the Japanese go even farther. In the electronics industry, for example, many small subcontractors farm out much of their work to even smaller firms or sometimes individual families. As we meet here today, approximately 180,000 Japanese are busy producing electronic components in their homes for these subcontractors, who in turn supply subassemblies to the major electronic manufacturing companies.

Small wonder, then, that the Sonys and the Matsushitas are able to keep their total labor costs low, even though their pay scales are now comparable to those in this country and Western Europe. And in the process millions of jobs are created for men and women who otherwise would probably be unemployed.

In the never-ending quest for greater productivity, the Japanese do not shy away from killing off dying products and industries. They are constantly asking themselves, "Is this the kind of product or industry in which we can be truly competitive? Or is this something we should get out of, so that we can use our capital and human resources more productively?"

Once dominant in transistor radios, the Japanese have happily forfeited that market to lower-labor-cost countries. They have replaced it with the higher-technology market of color television sets and, more recently, videotape recorders.

Such periodic product transitions are possible only because of the high educational level of the Japanese people. They "transplant" more easily into higher-technology jobs.

The "shape up or ship out" attitude, with which national planners view declining industries, is reinforced by Japan's financial structure. Commercial banks, which are the principal source of capital, simply refuse to finance a dying industry or company. Thus, it must either phase into more productive endeavors or eventually go out of business.

The quest for productivity is almost a national game. Far-out concepts are encouraged. Akio Morita, president of Sony, has said that he "loves to hear crazy ideas." And employees at Honda use their free time, plus company grants and facilities, to turn their dream inventions into reality—even the ones which Honda says "are only good for a laugh."

Consider the Choo-Choo cycle. It's a giant tricycle, on which the rider peddles furiously to generate electricity. This in turn heats a boiler, which in turn produces steam, which in turn powers what Honda describes as "the world's most inefficient vehicle."

To many Westerners, all this may seem rather silly. But for the Japanese, it obviously works. In addition to the industries I've already mentioned, the Japanese zeal for innovation and productivity works in audio equipment, musical instruments, bicycles, sports equipment, machine tools, photocopy machines, and many other products not commonly associated with Japanese culture or capabilities.

In only a few short years, Japan has become a competitor the like of which the world has not seen before. If we compare the competition for international markets with a football game—as seems appropriate here at Notre Dame—we must acknowledge that the Japanese have fielded quite a team. In fact, at this point the score is Japan 35 and the Western nations maybe 14.

Is the game in danger of turning into a rout? To answer that question let's do a little Monday-morning quarterbacking. Let's review what has happened here in the United States since the underrated team from the East began knocking the socks off the leader of the Western Conference.

Until the mid-1960s, the American economy towered above that of any other nation on earth. Yet in the past 15 years America's industrial engine has begun to knock, sputter, and display other alarming signs of impending breakdown.

Has this great economic engine been pushed too hard? Has it been poorly maintained? Has it been applied to the wrong tasks? Have we been trying to operate it on too lean a mixture? I believe the answer is yes to all these questions.

The truth is we have been careless caretakers of an economic system which for many decades created more wealth for more people than any other system in history. And the "we" includes all of us—government, labor, business management, and the public at large. It is the story of a legacy mismanaged—to such a degree that the United States faces the last two decades of this century with apprehension and fear.

Earlier, I referred to Japan's strong sense of national purpose and the willingness of the Japanese people to do what was necessary to achieve that country's goals. In contrast, the United States of the past decade has been a nation of sharply conflicting national goals.

Consider the role played by government: Under the delusion that government could guarantee every American a higher and higher standard of living every year, solve not only this country's social problems but also those of the rest of the world, and at the same time create a totally risk-free life for every citizen, the United States embarked on a bureaucratic crusade—at the national, state, and even local levels—which has been unprecedented in history. The cause was a noble one—no one disputes that. But unfortunately the Utopian dream was based on several false premises.

In the perspective of 1980, the most obvious miscalculations were (a) that the wealth of the United States was limitless and (b) that the economic engine would somehow run a little faster each year to compensate for the increasing demands being placed on it.

The scenario that followed is well known. I shall not dwell on it here, other than to point out that by the mid-1960s America's expectations began to substantially outrun its real output of goods and services. And to make up the difference, the federal government simply increased the supply of money.

Economist Paul Craig has pointed out that in all the years from the founding of the United States to the year 1966, the money supply grew from zero to 171 billion dollars. Yet today it has swollen to more than twice that—approximately 385 billion dollars. That is an increase of well over 200 billion dollars in 13 years.

During the same 13 years the federal deficit, not counting this year's deficit, has totaled 190 billion dollars. Dr. Craig suggests that the similarity of those figures—a federal deficit of 190 billion and the pouring of more than 200 billion into the money supply—is almost enough to make one develop a theory!

Yet even today, as the nation suffers under double-digit inflation which is on the verge of moving higher, we continue to hear from supposedly responsible public officials that OPEC is the root cause of America's inflation.

Suppose that whilst the printing presses at the Treasury were operating overtime, somehow the American economic engine had continued to run faster and faster each year—as it did in the 1950s and the early 1960s, when productivity gains were averaging 3 or 4 percent a year. Would that have made a difference?

It would have made a tremendous difference. But unfortunately, just the reverse happened. From 1968 to 1973 the annual productivity increase declined to less than 2 percent. Since 1973 it has averaged less than one percent. And for the past year and a half, productivity has actually declined. In the second quarter of 1980 the decline was approximately 3 percent.

That is not only crippling our output of goods and services; it is making America's products less competitive in markets abroad, which is one of the reasons the United States has lost 23 percent of its share of the world market in the past 10 years.

The dilemma of declining productivity, as you know, has been laid at many different doorsteps. We are frequently told that Americans have lost the will to work, and that coffee breaks, retirement parties and other social rituals, plus a high rate of absenteeism, have sapped the output of our factories and offices.

But my personal observation is that, on the whole, the American employee works as hard as his Japanese or German counterpart. So I think we have to probe deeper than that. And when we do, one conclusion is inevitable:

The productivity problem can be attributed primarily to

structural deficiencies in our current economic system rather than to any pronounced change in the traditional American work ethic.

Consider, for example, the area of industrial innovation. Perhaps more than any other factor, it was industrial innovation which made the United States the most productive nation on earth. Innovation created not only a wealth of new products and new services but entirely new industries.

The industry my own company is a part of—the computer systems industry—is a classic example. Thirty years ago, the computer was a laboratory curiosity; today, it has become a 100-billion-dollar business which during the 1980s is expected to become the world's fifth largest industry, exceeded only by the energy, automobile, steel, and chemical industries.

The computer industry—like nuclear power, aviation, television, instant photography, and satellite communications —is a high-technology industry spawned in America which grew out of this country's dedication to research and development.

Yet ever since the mid-1960s, the percentage of R&D spending to Gross National Product has been declining. Expenditures for basic R&D—the kind of research that gives birth to new industries—has dropped from 34 percent of total R&D allotments to only 25 percent today.

So far as R&D is concerned, we are like the farmer who every year sets aside a smaller amount of seed corn for the next year's crop, and then wonders why his production is falling off.

Comparable erosion has occurred in the American industrial plant. During the past 10 years many of America's factories have become obsolete or at best obsolescent. The average age of the machinery used in American plants today is 12 years. This compares with an average equipment age of seven years in the plants of our principal competitors.

We lag in automation as well. Japanese industry, with less than half the total output of American industry, has installed approximately 45,000 computer-controlled factory robots, compared with 5,000 here in the United States.

In this, the world's richest country, industry has been living on a low-calorie diet. The amount of capital invested per worker grew only 1.5 percent a year from 1963 to 1975. In Japan, the annual increase in capital investment per worker during the same period was 10.1 percent—seven times as much.

The tables have clearly turned; now it's the United States which must do the catching up—and on a massive scale. It's estimated that the U.S. steel industry alone needs to invest almost 5 billion dollars annually during the 1980s just to stay reasonably competitive with foreign steel producers.

What has happened to the American zeal for creating new ideas and opening new industrial frontiers? What has eroded this country's genius from producing more goods, more efficiently, for more people—generation after generation?

The causes of this industrial decline are, of course, legion. But it's suprising how many of the reasons for our current economic problems can be summed up in a single word. That word is "disincentive." In fact, I think it's fair to say that no other country has yet devised so many disincentives to innovation and productivity in such a short period of time.

In discussing these disincentives, I must reluctantly return to the role played by government. I say "reluctantly" because it is not my purpose—nor would it be fair—to make our elected officials the scapegoat for all of America's problems.

In the final analysis, a democratic government reflects the consensus, or lack of consensus, of the people it governs. And for the past decade the United States seemingly has lacked a sense of direction. Meanwhile, government has focused on ways to redistribute the wealth created by earlier generations, and to achieve through brute force the pet social engineering schemes of bureaucrats.

In pursuit of these nebulous objectives, government has:

—Engaged in a 15-year spending spree, which besides saddling the public with unprecedented inflation, has grossly distorted the earnings of business and industry. So much so that most of the profits being reported today are consumed in meeting the rising costs of staying in business, rather than in productive new investments.

—Government has also established a tax system which gives little incentive to business and industry to invest in R&D and new plants and equipment, and which simultaneously discourages personal savings.

—It has intervened in almost every phase of business operations with an endless maze of regulations which, by conservative estimates, are currently draining over 100 billion dollars a year from industry's basic function of providing goods and services.

—It has discouraged expansion by American business into overseas markets—by lack of any consistent trade policies, by ill-advised attempts to use exports as a club to force other countries to practice American concepts of morality, and by outmoded anti-trust laws which effectively prevent many American companies from competing successfully with powerful foreign consortiums.

The list of indictments could go on and on. As economist Lester Thurow has pointed out, the U.S. economy today is bleeding from "a thousand cuts."

I wish it were possible to say that business is blameless in this multiple, persistent wounding of the economy. But such is not the case.

Most business leaders have been quick to unmask the folly of much of the legislation of recent years. However, we have been less than adept in preparing our own companies for the winds of change which began sweeping through almost every industry in the 1970s.

—We have allowed our plants to turn out too many shoddy products under the mistaken impression that the consumer will buy anything so long as it's made in the U.S.A.

—We have tended to subordinate long-range planning to short-range expediency.

—We have devoted too much time and too many resources to

shoring up eroding markets, and have not paid enough attention to emerging new markets.

—We have preached about the need to keep the spirit of enterprise alive, but we've often been overly cautious when the time came to actually put our chips on the board.

—And all the while, we have reassured ourselves as to the wisdom of our course by reporting record revenues and earnings. We have chosen to ignore the realistic dictum of management consultant Peter Drucker that in an inflationary environment, "the figures lie."

And what of organized labor? Again, labor—along with government and business—must accept a share of the blame for America's industrial decline.

As the experience of Japan has demonstrated, labor has as much at stake in achieving improved productivity as management, or the nation as a whole. Yet many unions continue to fight tooth and nail against productivity-enhancing changes. Instead, they have clung tenaciously to outmoded work practices that narrowly define who can do what—when, where, and how. In many industries these rigid work rules have locked companies into a style of operation which is totally inadequate for meeting the competitive realities of today.

Along with government and much of business, labor has also succumbed to the illusion that America's economic growth is an automatic, never-ending process. The overriding philosophy at the bargaining table has been to squeeze the last drop out of the bottle and to let someone else worry about how the bottle is to be refilled.

This "pass-along-the-problem" approach is nowhere more evident than in the cost-of-living provisions written into labor contracts covering millions of employees—provisions which have helped increase hourly labor costs in the auto industry, as only one example, by 20 percent in the past year alone. Yet we are now hearing cries of bewilderment over the unprecedented influx of Japanese-built autos in the U.S. market, at a time when over 200,000 American auto workers are out of work.

Many years ago, the historian Edward Gibbon explained

the decline and fall of the ancient city of Athens in a few chilling words. He said:

In the end, more than they wanted freedom, they wanted security. They wanted a comfortable life. And in their quest for it all—security, comfort and freedom—they lost it all. When the Athenians wanted finally not to give to society, but for society to give to them; when the freedom they wished for most, was the freedom from responsibility, then Athens ceased to be free.

Can the United States escape a similar fate? I believe that depends, in large measure, on whether this country can regain the competitive edge it has lost in recent years.

Certainly the first step in meeting the economic challenge posed by Japan and other international competitors is to recognize the seriousness of the problem. And evidence is mounting daily that Americans in all walks of life are indeed aware that the nation's industrial engine badly needs a major overhaul.

The message has even reached Washington. As the presidential and congressional campaigns begin building to a peak, each of the presidential candidates—along with every other office-seeker—has sensed the deep concern throughout America about the future direction of the economy.

Almost overnight, "reindustrialization" has become the buzzword of 1980. It is now a favorite theme not only of candidates for political office, but of television specials, radio talk shows, articles in prestigious magazines, town meetings, and even discussions at cocktail parties.

Many liberals are beginning to sound like conservatives. And conservatives are as pleasantly surprised as a professor who discovers at the end of a long lecture that his class has actually paid attention to what he's been saying.

This is all very encouraging. But catchy phrases and red, white, and blue bumper stickers proclaiming the national will to revitalize the American economy will not solve the economic problems which have been building for 15 years.

It is regrettable, but true, that the mammoth rebuilding task everybody is talking about will require making some hard choices—by government, by business, and by labor.

Also, by the tens of millions of other Americans, young and old, who are not part of the power structure.

On November 4th—after the bands have stopped playing, and the last of the campaign oratory has faded away—will the national consensus on the need for rebuilding America's industrial base also begin to fade away in the face of those hard choices? That, of course, is the unanswerable question.

We must proceed, however, on the assumption that the American people—like the Japanese people 35 years ago—will in fact demonstrate a willingness to do what is necessary to breathe new life into the national economy. Certainly that is the one mandatory requirement for reversing the United States' economic decline.

The dilemma facing America today transcends the issue of meeting the Japanese economic challenge—important as that issue is. The Japanese challenge is but the tip of the iceberg; it is highly visible because of the 9-billion-dollar trade deficit with Japan anticipated for this year, and because Japanese-made products are flooding the American marketplace.

But the bulk of the iceberg is still unperceived in many quarters. It is not only Japan which is challenging America's traditional leadership in scores of industries; it is other industrialized countries as well, plus many lean and hungry developing countries.

I'm not suggesting that the Japanese challenge should be underestimated, or that the Japanese experience is without lessons for the United States. It is indeed the most pressing challenge of the moment, and we can benefit by emulating a number of Japanese practices. But we cannot expect Americans to behave like Japanese. Japan is a highly homogenized society, with a history and a culture which are alien to the history and culture of the United States. It is basically a group-oriented society, whilst the United States has been, and remains, essentially individual-oriented.

It seems to me therefore that America's response, both to the Japanese challenge and the broader worldwide challenge, must be built on American strengths, American values, and the American political and social structure.

Business Week magazine has defined the challenge in the most succinct terms I have seen. The United States, it says, must develop a

consensus-forming framework under which government, business, labor, and other interest groups—without compromising their traditional goals—can agree on tradeoffs that would both strengthen the economy and, in the end, prove beneficial to all.

I think we would all agree that government must be the chief architect in designing and developing such a framework. It is the country's elected officials, and the governmental departments they control, who must establish the necessary priorities. It is government which must create a favorable environment for such an effort.

The public mandate for overhauling the world's largest economy is unmistakably clear. What is less clear is whether government is equal to the task. Admittedly, it will be a task of awesome complexity.

—As a first step, it will require a major shifting of governmental emphasis, including the slowing down of attempts to create an egalitarian society and the speeding up of efforts to generate economic growth. To achieve this massive redirection, government will have to greatly increase its planning and coordinating capabilities.

—It will also require acceptance of the fact that any viable program to rebuild the national economy must reduce, to some extent, the level of personal consumption during the initial years of the revitalization effort. There are no magical recipes for creating a larger pie overnight. If a larger slice of the Gross National Product is to be allotted to productive investment, each of the remaining slices of the pie will have to be reduced accordingly. And that must start at the governmental level—specifically with a meaningful reduction in the federal budget and corresponding monetary restraint—reinforced by comparable fiscal restraint by state and local governments.

—Any successful rebuilding effort must also recognize the futility of trying to prop up low-skilled, labor-intensive industries, whose products must compete with comparable products manufactured at a fraction of the U.S. cost in low-wage developing countries. Here, too, a change in emphasis will be required—away from traditional attempts to increase blue-collar employment and toward the creation of new jobs in knowledge-intensive industries. This will necessitate major investments in job retraining programs, and, at a more basic level, reorientation of the nation's educational system.

—The rebuilding program will also require a concentrated effort to increase America's exports. This includes the establishment of appropriate export incentives and the removal of current disincentives, plus a revision of anti-trust laws so that American versions of the highly successful Japanese trading companies can open new markets abroad.

—Most important of all, it will require greater stimulation of research and development to create new products, new industries, and new jobs and greater capital investment in new plants and equipment so that those products—and existing products—can be manufactured more efficiently than their counterparts abroad.

I've listed several philosophical concepts which in my view are necessary if government is to serve as the catalyst for reversing the recent slippage of the U.S. economy. These concepts are, of course, easier stated than implemented. And their implementation would be viewed with varying degrees of enthusiasm by various interest groups.

Yet on one phase of their implementation there appears to be widespread agreement; namely, that increased investment is the indispensable key for unlocking America's potential for economic growth. The problem is not only to accelerate the rate of capital formation, but to make sure that the additional capital flows into productive channels.

The most powerful tool for achieving those objectives is tax reform—to be specific, tax reform in three primary areas:

First, current tax laws should be amended to provide meaningful incentives to spur research and development. Studies show that high-technology industries generate triple the growth rate, twice the productivity rate, and nine times the employment growth of low-technology industries. America has long been the world leader in high technology. That leadership is now in jeopardy, primarily because R&D expenditures, as a percentage of Gross National Product, have shown virtually no real growth in the past 10 years.

Second, current tax laws should be revised to permit more rapid depreciation of capital investments in new plants and equipment. Current depreciation schedules are inconsistent with the real world—not only because replacement costs have soared, but because of the speed with which most industries, especially high-technology industries, are changing. As only one example, my own company will have to invest almost 400 million dollars in the 1980s to stay competitive in semiconductors, which are the basic building blocks of computers and other types of information-processing equipment.

Third, current tax laws should be amended so as to stimulate personal savings instead of personal consumption. The United States stands unique among industrial nations in penalizing the thrifty and rewarding those who live beyond their means. With an inflation rate twice that of the allowable interest on savings accounts, and with dividends and most other investments subject to double taxation, it is remarkable that Americans save anything at all. The effect of this is further dilution of the capital available for economic growth.

In correcting these glaring deficiencies in the current tax structure, we need only to look to our international competitors for guidance. Japan, for example, offers special depreciation allowances for new technology investments. Canada provides a 10 percent investment tax credit for all research and development expenditures. Germany, France, and the United Kingdom permit accelerated depreciation for both plant and equipment used in scientific and technical research. Comparable incentives are offered by those countries to encourage plant modernization and the growth of personal savings.

Just as we need to generate more capital for investment, so we need to reduce the flow of capital into non-productive areas. Few would quarrel with the good intentions of most of the regulatory legislation of recent years. Protecting the environment, eliminating on-the-job health and safety hazards, and ensuring equal opportunity employment are as justifiable from a business viewpoint as they are from a social or humanitarian viewpoint.

What cannot be justified—or tolerated if the United States is to remain a strong international competitor—is the tragic waste, inefficiency, and inconsistency which characterize so many government regulations today.

It is indeed an Alice-In-Wonderland world when one arm of government is constantly pushing for greater use of pesticides at the same time another agency is restricting their use; or when one branch of the federal bureaucracy is demanding weight-adding safety features for automobiles even as another agency is promoting lighter-weight cars to reduce gasoline consumption. A visitor from another planet might well conclude that we have all gone mad.

Not long ago the Business Roundtable sponsored a study of costs incurred by 48 companies in complying with the regulations of only six federal agencies. Those costs amounted to 16 percent of the companies' net income and 43 percent of their expenditures for research and development.

Clearly, it is time for government to begin weighing the merits of many existing regulations and all proposed new regulations against the drain they cause on the capital needed to rejuvenate the national economy.

Rebuilding America's economy will also test the ability of business managers to develop better policies and practices than those that were followed in the 1970s. In the 1980s we need to raise our sights beyond this month's sales report and this year's financial performance. We need to be more interested in where our companies will be five years from now than where they are today. And we must begin measuring our own performances as business managers, and the performances of our subordinates, in terms of contributions to long-term growth and increased market penetration as well as short-term profits.

And that will be difficult. To quote philosopher Paul Valery, "The trouble with our times is that the future is not what it used to be."

I, for one, hope that the future truly will not be what it used to be, insofar as the traditional adversary relationship of business and labor is concerned. If American products are to regain the preeminence they once enjoyed in the international marketplace, we shall have to develop new approaches to that relationship—approaches that will help refurbish this country's reputation for technologically-advanced, high-quality products manufactured with pride and efficiency.

Earlier this month a Japanese trade delegation flew to Detroit, ostensibly to buy auto parts from U.S. manufacturers, but also to pour oil on the troubled waters caused by record exports of Japanese-made cars to this country. The delegation brought along a statement from the managing director of Japan's largest auto manufacturer. It warned the American parts suppliers that they had better improve the quality of their products or face the loss of any future business from Japan.

The fact that this could, and did happen—in what Americans have always regarded as the auto capital of the world—points up the magnitude of the task confronting American management and labor in the 1980s. It was a classic case of role reversal, with the once-vaunted U.S. auto industry and its suppliers reduced to the status one might give a fledgling industry in some remote banana republic.

I find it difficult to believe that either American management or American labor will be willing to accept that kind of secondary economic role in the world economy of the 1980s. I don't think anyone in government wants it either. Yet there is a clear and present danger that this could happen in many other industries as well. It seems to me that is the real essence of the economic challenge that faces this country.

Can the trend be reversed? In my judgment it can be.

It is true that Japan, to use today's vernacular, seemingly

"has it made." But is the Japanese position in tomorrow's economic world really that secure?

—More than any other industrial country, Japan is highly vulnerable to future disruptions in the supply of oil and other basic resources, as global political tensions continue to mount.

—Japan today is also a high-labor-cost country. It, too, must convert its present industrial base into one that is more heavily weighted toward higher-technology, higher-valued-added products. As the Ministry of International Trade and Industry recently noted, "The period when Japan made progress by applying and improving existing ideas has already come to an end, and a period of creativity and initiative is beginning."

—Also, increasing trade friction has raised the spectre of anti-Japanese protectionism in both the United States and Europe, which are Japan's principal markets. And even if international trade remains relatively free, Japan will have to vastly increase its direct investment abroad to remain competitive in many markets. Doing so will require huge amounts of capital. Also, it raises the question of how transplantable the Japanese success formula will be in other countries.

—In addition, Japan's own internal house is not in the best of order. Rising inflation, substandard housing, growing consumerism, and the need to streamline an unwieldy state bureaucracy are problems which the Japanese have not yet solved.

—Finally, there are signs that the Japanese people themselves, having achieved a level of affluence that once was only dreamed about, are moving toward a somewhat different lifestyle. It is a lifestyle that envisions more leisure time, greater emphasis on culture, and—Heaven forbid—perhaps even doing nothing at all productive once in a while!

The fact that Japan is entering the 1980s with its own agenda of difficult problems offers scant solace to the United States. Momentum still favors the Japanese.

But it's now apparent that the United States—which in

recent years has often appeared to be the sleeping giant of the
world's industrial nations—is beginning to wake up at last.
And although the scoreboard at the moment may read 35 to
14, the home team still has time to revise its game plan, beef
up its offense, and win the big one after all.

It should be an interesting second half.

ORGANIZED LABOR IN THE 1980s: THE PUSH FOR UNIFICATION[1]

Nick Thimmesch[2]

Less than a week before the inauguration of Ronald Reagan,
Nick Thimmesch, columnist for the Los Angeles Times Syndicate,
author, frequent panelist on "Meet the Press," "Face the Nation,"
and other televised public affairs programs, addressed the fifth annual Political Action Committee Conference in Washington, D.C.,
on January 14, 1981. The conference was sponsored by the Public
Affairs Council, a non-profit, bipartisan professional organization
of corporate public affairs executives.

Thimmesch's audience of approximately one hundred leaders
and staff members of various political action committees was assembled in a public meeting room in the Hyatt Regency Hotel.
Aware that many of those present were deeply concerned about
how the approaching inauguration of a conservative Republican
President would affect the future, Thimmesch chose to speak on
the topic, "Organized Labor in the 1980s: the Push for Unification." The columnist prefaced his discussion of the future of the
labor movement with a review of the evolution of organized labor
in America up to date, emphasizing changes which had altered the
public's perception of unions and labor union problems. He then
turned to the future, saying,

I am not going to declare that the 1980 elections marked
the year that the American labor movement went into permanent decline or even suffered its greatest shock. But after talk-

---

[1] Delivered to the fifth annual Political Action Committee Conference, Washington,
D.C., at 11:15 A.M. on January 14, 1981.
[2] For biographical note, see Appendix.

ing personally to a number of top labor leaders, surveying the reaction in their usually brash publications and taking some soundings, I believe that it is fair to say that organized labor admits it took a drubbing the 1980 elections. . . . Clearly, the labor movement can't be bullish about itself going into 1981. It faces an unfriendly Senate, a less sympathetic House, and an unobligated Reagan administration.

Thimmesch began his speech at 11:15 A.M. Noting that the conference had been hearing speeches since 8:30 A.M., he told them, "I shall talk for about 25 minutes and then take your questions. After that, you get lunch and more speeches and workshops." "This conference," he declared, "is loaded with the work ethic."

The address clearly reveals that Thimmesch is a skilled speaker with a facility for incorporating humor to create good will and establish rapport with his listeners. The columnist did not come by this ability by chance. Although he did not major in speech at the University of Iowa, Thimmesch was a student of the distinguished speech teacher and scholar, A. Craig Baird, who served as editor of *Representative American Speeches,* from 1937 to 1959. Thimmesch credits Baird, one of the great teachers of rhetoric and public address in this century, with having a great influence on his life.

I am delighted to be here. From the program I gather you have been diligently concentrating and perhaps sitting since 8:30 in the morning and hearing leftists and rightists alike, so, if you would like to stand up and stretch, please do so.

I am complimented that you invited me to speak at this political action committee conference. But, do I have to make a donation? I truly am a political independent—a philosophical militant moderate.

Before we plunge into this thing, my topic being "Organized Labor in the 1980s," I want to observe that next Tuesday in this town, the jellybean will replace the peanut as a favorite snack item. So invest in jellybeans.

My friend Mark Russell says that after Mr. Reagan announced what he was going to wear to the inauguration, and it was rather formal indeed, 300 Congressmen quietly returned their white socks to Tuxedo rental shops. Mark also claims that the new Republican leisure suit is an oxford-gray stroller jacket, gray striped trousers, a vest, and a four-in-hand gray, striped tie.

Anyway, I hope that Mr. Reagan takes naps in the afternoon. I hope he keeps riding his horse. And I hope he buys back the Presidential yacht, the Sequoia, although I know he'll have to pay double for what Jimmy sold it for. By now, maybe Billy owns it.

I plan to talk for about 25 minutes and then take your questions. After that, you get lunch and more speeches and workshops. This conference is loaded with the work ethic.

It is useful, in looking at organized labor in the '80s, to briefly outline the evolution of the American labor movement. As a movement, it is relatively young. While there were unions, crafts and guilds through American history, it wasn't until 1881—100 years ago—that the Federation of Organized Trades & Labor Movements was founded. Five years later, Samuel Gompers transformed this nucleus organization into the American Federation of Labor. The old AFL was interested in better pay, shorter work weeks, and improved working conditions. The closest it ever came to being ideological was the Gompers doctrine of rewarding its friends and punishing its enemies. The AFL was very bourgeois.

It wasn't until the mid-'30s, when the CIO was formed, partly from dissenting AFL industrial unions, that big labor went ideological. John L. Lewis, Walter Reuther, and Philip Murray—these were the titans of industrial unionism. They devised the powerful political action committee—an original PAC? After years of warring, and only after the CIO had expelled communists from its ranks, the AFL and CIO merged in 1955, with P.A.C. becoming the Committee on Political Education, still powerful.

The AFL-CIO was strong from the beginning, but was not without its tumult and shouting. In 1957, the AFL-CIO expelled three affiliates charged with corruption, most notably Dave Beck and Jimmy Hoffa's teamsters. Years later, the United Auto Workers quit the AFL-CIO, mostly because Reuther didn't like George Meany.

But even when unions threw their weight around in the

'50s and '60s, when they were enormously successful in electing "their" people to public office, and when they built huge strike and supplemental unemployment benefit funds and union treasuries, and when many Americans came to fear and even dislike unions, there were changes under way in the American economy which would thwart and limit unions as much as any counterattack by management or political opponents.

The changes were automation, the explosion in the service industry, the decline of ideology in American working people, and the relentless shift of population and wealth from the Northeast and Midwest to the South, Southwest and West.

Moreover, the going got rough for union organizers in these booming regions, and the old industrial unions began losing members. At the end of World War II, one of every three American workers belonged to a labor union. Today it's one in every four. The figure is headed for one in five in the '80s. A few years ago, for the first time, organized labor actually recorded a numerical loss of membership.

If this wasn't enough, the rest of the world became skillful in manufacturing goods, and began beating out American industry in many markets. This caused U.S. corporations to not only flee the old industrial and unionized areas for the South, but for overseas sanctuaries which couldn't be touched by U.S. unions.

Where in the '30s spies and company goons intimidated and physically assaulted aggressive unionists, management got smart. Sharp lawyers and human relations specialists now team up with public relations men to talk employees into the notion that they don't really need to belong to a labor union to succeed in America.

Union leaders didn't want to admit it, but they had sailed into a Sargasso Sea. Much of the labor movement had become stagnant. The only growth that unions experienced was in the service industry, in education with the militant National Education Association, and in the public sector, with government employees. Once, the United Steel Workers were the largest union in the AFL-CIO. Today, it is the American Federation of State, County, and Municipal Employees, with well over a million members.

The aging leaders of the union movement focused more on pensions, job protection, the Office of Safety and Health Administration, their salt-free diets and spreading waistlines. More and more, we heard about union members in crafts that were being automated, like printers and linotype operators, taking early retirement and thousands and thousands of bucks as a sweetened inducement. Even the poor old mailmen of the Postal Service are being replaced by automation. The ranks of the postal workers will soon be only two-thirds of what they were three years ago. The people who made shoes in New England factories learned what Italian- and Spanish-made shoes were. The garment workers in midtown Manhattan found out about fingers of Asians skilled with needles and machines which make clothes. Must I even mention Detroit automakers and Japan, or Pittsburgh and foreign steel?

Still, there are impressive, monument-type buildings in Washington where the union movement headquarters, and where politicians pay their courtesy calls, and where union chieftains preside. Organized labor, in 1981, remains a key factor in our economy, and played a substantial role in the long, tedious process by which decreasing numbers of Americans select presidential candidates and others as well—and finally elect them in November.

I am not going to declare that the 1980 elections marked the year that the American labor movement went into permanent decline, or experienced its greatest loss in prestige and power, or even suffered its greatest shock. But after talking personally to a number of top labor leaders, surveying the reaction in their usually brash union publications, and taking some soundings, I believe that it is fair to say that organized labor admits it took a drubbing in the 1980 elections.

"Americans expressed a desire for change" was the softly offered explanation of Lane Kirkland, President of the AFL-CIO. Douglas A. Fraser, President of the beleagured United Auto Workers, remarked that "maybe it's time to turn to different ideas"—quite an admission from the president of a union which was always so sure of itself.

The union chieftains now talk about "regrouping," "unification," broader involvement in politics, particularly primaries, and a bigger say-so on company actions affecting what the chieftains regard as the vital interest of their members.

Organized labor does not talk about getting tough with the Reagan administration.

Clearly, the labor movement can't be bullish about itself going into 1981. It faces an unfriendly Senate, a less sympathetic House, and an unobligated Reagan administration.

As labor goes into the '80s, it intensifies its effort to protect jobs. The United Auto Workers joined the Ford Motor Company and Chrysler in calling for federal government restraints on Japanese automakers, and also asked Japan to increase the "local content" of cars sold in the United States. The U.A.W., sounding like your favorite Chevy, Ford, Plymouth or American Motors dealer, runs advertisements urging Americans to at least test drive a U.S.-built car before buying a foreign one.

Yes, labor in the '80s is hunkering down. It is long past the time when it could indulge itself in "featherbedding" or archaic make-work practices. There is no more Brotherhood of Locomotive Firemen. There is no more "dead horse," setting the Bible in the backshop at a newspaper, just to put in hours. And on the waterfront, where is Marlon Brando??? Old longshoremen never die, they just fade away—with a guarantee of $20,000 a year for life.

Union leaders today cling to the Davis-Bacon law. It requires Federal contractors to pay "prevailing" union wages, and makes it easier for such contractors to deal with unions.

In what Abe Raskin, a man who understands the labor movement as well as anyone in the Republic, calls "push-button unionism," some big unions use a device to avoid the struggle of following companies moving south or west. These unions, and the United Auto Workers is one, exact a pledge from a company to allow its new plant in a "union-free environment" to be readily organized. Thus the union rides with company executives—a free ride, so to speak.

"We *own* the jobs," is what Steve Schlossberg, the United

Auto Workers director of governmental and public affairs, insisted to me in no uncertain terms, and with a bit of bravery in his voice. "We can't have all these plant closings and re-movals to the sunbelt and Third World." He talked of the great loss of homes, medical benefits and community institu-tions. He talked about "revitalization" to save all this.

"Revitalization" was much chattered about by union leaders before the election. This term, if not the need, has gone with the wind and Jimmy Carter. The union leaders hoped vainly, as they did with the toothless Humphrey-Haw-kins law, that the Federal government would establish an-other programmatic panacea.

But the prospect is that though Ronald Reagan got 44 percent of the vote of union members, the new administra-tion's concept of "revitalization" will be to subtract, rather than add, government programs and regulations. The deregu-lation process will be accelerated under the new administra-tion. And on Capitol Hill, the new chairman of the Senate Labor & Human Resources Committee, Orrin G. Hatch—a onetime union member himself—has raised the prospect of repealing the Davis-Bacon law.

The labor leaders I talked with in the past couple of weeks told me that they weren't so afraid of what Reagan might do to them, as what the new Congress would try to do. The two-tier minimum wage—which labor wags crack is not enough to buy two beers—is regarded as a major threat. This is the proposal which would establish an entry-level minimum wage for teenagers, and retain the present minimum wage for other workers. Some people call it the McDonald's restaurant relief bill—I don't know.

Anyway, the unions are bracing themselves for withering blasts from employers and other conservative elements invig-orated by the election results. Senator Jake Garn has a special gimlet eye focused on OSHA. Employers talk about pressing for reform of unemployment compensation laws which they regard as cost-excessive. If that isn't enough bad news from the Hill, there are Senator Jesse Helms and Congressman John Erlenborn pushing to prohibit use of union dues for "po-litical education." And so it goes.

The lively, sometimes feisty right-to-work movement now claims 1.6 million members, and that's a quantum jump for them. Egads, they have 38,000 members in Arkansas alone. Well, this movement points to 20 right-to-work states, and is saying that Idaho and New Mexico will be next.

Unions have railed against right-to-work for so long that they sound hoarse on the subject. But at a time when unionism is weak, such counterattacks only sap more strength. So in the '80s, unions increasingly work to conserve what they have. Unions have long called for the right to have a voice in how the hundreds of billions of dollars in pension plans are administered. Now they are speaking in a lower but just as determined voice, and are asking for a greater role.

One official of the AFL-CIO told me: "We want to make sure that such (pension fund) investment serves a social purpose like worker housing and health centers. We also want that money used to reindustrialize so that we can get more jobs. And we don't want it invested in non- or anti-union companies."

That sounds like bread and butter unionism, with a senior citizen slant. But some unionists, and they are few, talk blue sky about unions being brought into the planning and management of major industries. My friend Schlossberg at the U.A.W. described the idea of a "new social compact" for America, in terms of the economy.

"We can't run this country with pristine-pure Milton Friedman economics," he told me. "General Motors wouldn't dream of beginning this decade without planning, so why shouldn't the whole country?"

True, this kind of brotherhood between management and labor is practiced in some European countries. Sweden seems to go for it, and one lesson some American companies are learning is that the Japanese do very well by sending their top management into the plant to sit down with workers and ask them in friendly fashion, What the hell is going on? Are things being done right? And what should be done to improve the operation of the company? By the way, the New York *Times Magazine* of January 4 had an excellent article on this subject.

But for every 10 minutes a union leader will spend telling you about management's shortcomings—as though the union man is secretly aspiring to be a manager himself—he won't give you much time on the question of improving productivity. Union chieftains are only easing into the productivity discussion. The Auto Workers are almost brave about it.

I might mention here that while Auto Workers President Doug Fraser is a certified member of a company board of directors—Chrysler—I can't find a rush of other union chieftains who think it is good for them to serve on such boards. The wise men at the AFL-CIO still see the management-labor relationship as one of adversaries.

If union leadership is disinterested in sitting on corporate boards, it is very interested in "unifying" the retrenched labor movement. Lane Kirkland talks grandly of "unification in the 1980s," meaning he wants to bring the Teamsters and Mine Workers back into the AFL-CIO fold. When he is asked about possible corruption in the Teamsters, Kirkland sounds like a born-again. He urges understanding, and says, "We're not a lynch mob."

Surely, Kirkland is thinking that with industrial unions losing members fast, and with the Teamsters displaying success in organizing the fast-growing service industry, still largely non-union, such tolerance of an old sinner is virtuous and practical as well.

The retail field . . . . Montgomery Ward . . . . Sears . . . . and a million lost fast food joints . . . . are ripe to be more extensively organized, and Kirkland knows that. "All sinners belong in church," he cracks. "All unions belong in the AFL-CIO." Again, conservation, consolidation—hunkering down with the better-off Teamsters, if need be.

The public service unions, those representing local, state and federal employees, are doing very well. But they grow and prosper at a time when their employers, the taxpayers, are rebelling against the cost of government. So the more these unions push for raises and benefits in the '80s, the more propositions are going to wind up on the ballot—from Proposition 13 to 2½ in Taxachusetts and beyond.

Whenever Lane Kirkland talks glowingly of the coming "unification"—"getting everybody back in church," somebody brings up that curious cult called the National Education Association. Kirkland always politely calls them a "special problem," and reminds one and all that the AFL-CIO has within its ranks the American Federation of Teachers. But the N.E.A., with its 2.1 million members, dwarfs the A.F.T. Moreover, the N.E.A., despite its alliance with Jimmy Carter, is not going back to Plains with him.

This is perhaps the most militant union in the Republic, and also the most clever. The N.E.A. doesn't always admit to being a union. In some states, it prefers wearing the hat of a teachers' professional association. In those areas where unionism is still strong, the N.E.A. is a good old trade union. I look for the N.E.A. to continue in the '80s as a strong labor union—a potent, feared political force, and perhaps even a major ideological influence in our society. They have so many built-in advantages.

Now, what to say about organized labor and its political role in the months and years ahead? Number One: I don't see the labor movement as starting a quick fight with the new administration. There just isn't enough public support for unionism these days to sustain any such effort.

Organized labor has shown no inclination to even challenge the nomination of Ray Donovan as Secretary of Labor. One union skate called him "a hard negotiator, but fair," and that's about the consensus. I heard favorable comparisons of Donovan with Eisenhower's Secretary of Labor, James Mitchell. I repeat: Labor is more leery of the Hill than of Reagan in the White House.

This doesn't mean that labor is going to lie low politically. Kirkland and other chieftains believe that they goofed on the political front in recent elections. And this brings me to Number 2: The decision that labor is now making to get involved in the primaries. Historically, they have avoided primaries, but the political process today makes the primaries on all levels particularly potent.

So I look for organized labor to plunge into the 1982 pri-

maries, take sides, and eventually beat the drum for the kind
of Democratic presidential nominee they want in 1984.

Number 3: I see labor unions playing a widening role as
social critic. Unions have used the "working conditions" issue
not only to point out environmental jeopardies to workers on
the job, but they have gone beyond into the workers' day-to-
day living environment as well. Unions today want to discuss
and argue the energy question, the right to decision-making
on productivity, and even the definition of what is the "work
ethic."

Altogether, this is a different labor movement from what
we knew 10 or 20 years ago, and certainly what existed 100
years ago when labor concentrated its strength into one organization.

Today, when fringe benefits account for up to 40 percent
of workers' income, dollars and cents bargaining centers
mostly on holding the cost of living allowance.

The great concern of organized labor today is to hold—
hold onto jobs, membership, pensions, special arrangements
like Davis-Bacon, and even the movement itself. Hence the
push for unification.

Organized labor today is still plenty strong, and in some
districts and regions packs political clout. But labor realizes it
must take a new direction in politics. It must win a bigger
say-so in the Democratic Party, and help shape that party in
more traditional terms.

The more adventuresome in labor today talk about "social
concepts," and sharing in management's decisions.

Now, having surveyed the American labor movement as it
goes into the '80s, let me say that, for better or worse, a capitalistic, enterprise system must have a labor movement. We
need that adversary relationship to keep balance. This might
sound heretical to some in this audience, but I believe it. And
we need a few heretics in this vail of tears. Thank you very
much. I am ready for your questions, barbs, missiles or whatever.

EDUCATION IN THE 80s

HIGHER EDUCATION IN THE 80s: BEYOND RETRENCHMENT[1]

JOHN C. SAWHILL[2]

The American Association of Higher Education, founded in 1870, is an organization of faculty members, administrators, trustees, public officials, and interested individuals from all segments of post-secondary education. Its purpose is to clarify and help resolve crucial issues in college and university education through conferences, publications, and special meetings.

On March 6, 1980, John C. Sawhill, then Deputy Secretary in the Department of Energy, addressed the organization's National Conference on Higher Education in Washington, D.C. The speech was delivered at 2 P.M. at one of the approximately 75 sessions of the annual conference to an audience of between 400 and 500 members in the International Ballroom East of the Washington Hilton Hotel.

Dr. Sawhill was admirably qualified to discuss higher education in the 1980s. Although working for the government at the time, he was on leave from his post as president of New York University, the largest private university in the country. Associates describe him as "a quick study, able to absorb enormous amounts of information and inevitably the best-prepared person at every meeting he attends, . . . a man who gets passionate about things," and someone with a flair for drama. (New York *Times Magazine*, Ap. 30, '78) Sawhill is six feet tall and has been described as having broad shoulders, long strong fingers, and—as a result of his jogging—not an ounce of fat on his 145-pound frame. His hair is dark and hangs over his ears in a somewhat shaggy fashion, but otherwise he is a "neatnik."

Early in his address, Dr. Sawhill expressed concern over the kind of thinking of some educators concerning the 1980s, saying:

[1] Delivered at the American Association of Higher Education's annual National Conference on Higher Education, International Ballroom East, Washington Hilton Hotel, Washington, D.C., at 2 P.M., on March 6, 1980.
[2] For biographical note, see Appendix.

I find it disturbing that there are those who see the process of self-scrutiny and reassessment that universities are currently going through as nothing more than "retrenchment"—a kind of educational equivalent to fiscal belt-tightening and budget-shearing. A going backwards if you will. . . . Talk of "retrenchment" only makes sense if we accept an austere, minimalist view of the kind of curricular change that we need.

I do not endorse such a view. The world around us, and consequently our educative mission, grows more complex and more rapidly moving with each year. We cannot replicate courses and prescribe educational experiences that were appropriate to the world of the 1930s or the 1950s. What we must seek is new ways to conceptualize and integrate knowledge. Any general education curriculum that fails to meet this challenge is doomed to obsolescence before it has hatched.

Sawhill's approach to this topic is interesting. In contrast to the broad, philosophical forecasts regarding education in the '80s by many educators, Sawhill chose to discuss many specific concerns, such as expository writing, computer usage, foreign languages, survey courses, teaching the classics, non-Western cultural studies, the natural sciences, and law.

This year, almost two-and-a-half million new students embarked on their first steps of higher education. By the time they graduate as the class of 1983, universities, which tend to progress in almost imperceptible steps, must define and redirect the course and quality of higher education to meet the challenges of a rapidly changing society, as well as the needs of students who will have to cope creatively and constructively with an energy transition that will introduce the ethics of conservation and sacrifice into the American lifestyle.

There is a great debate going on in the country today over what should be the purpose, the spirit, and the goals of undergraduate education. As we move into the 1980s, faculty and administrators at colleges and universities are arguing, revising, and updating their liberal arts curricula. As president (on leave) of the largest, private urban institution in the nation, I know that it is an enormous job; certainly it rivals my current position at the Department of Energy. But whatever the merits and the shape of any particular university's final curriculum plan, the current debate is raising our national consciousness as educators, students, and parents; it is making us evaluate what is worth teaching our young men and women, what needs preserving, and what can safely be jettisoned.

I find it disturbing that there are those who see the process of self-scrutiny and reassessment that universities are currently going through as nothing more than "retrenchment"—a kind of educational equivalent to fiscal belt-tightening and budget-shearing. A going backwards if you will, from some of the more daring educational experiments of the last few decades and particularly the 1960s. We are indeed hearing much talk about "going back to basics," but this trend, I believe, though important, represents only a small part of what is needed.

Talk of "retrenchment" only makes sense if we accept an austere, minimalist view of the kind of curricular change that we need. I do not endorse such a view. The world around us, and consequently our educative mission, grows more complex, and more rapidly moving, with each year. We cannot replicate courses and prescribe educational experiences that were appropriate to the world of the 1930s or the 1950s. What we must seek is new ways to conceptualize and integrate knowledge. Any general education curriculum that fails to meet this challenge is doomed to obsolescence before it has hatched.

It is inconceivable to me that any general education proposal would not have a contemporary dimension. Students have a right—and faculty members an obligation—to grapple with the "relevant" pressing social and scientific concerns of our time. Indeed, so long as social relevance is not confused with shallow trendiness and is not used as a stick to beat those faculty members whose job it is to pass on traditional subjects—say Victorian literature or the Philosophy of the Enlightenment—I am all for it.

Further in the vein of relevance, universities and colleges must take decisive steps toward insuring that our literate pop-

ulation is more generally competent in the use and compre-
hension of foreign languages and in the sounder and more
sympathetic understanding of foreign cultures.

And, it is precisely on the grounds of social relevance that
we support the addition of computer science to the mathe-
matics requirement that exists at most major universities. A
basic understanding of computer usage and some familiarity
with one of the computer languages is essential for the educated college graduate of the 1980s.

It may be true, as the distinguished scientist Lewis
Thomas suggests, that the *mystique* of computers is too great
and that to use his words, "no one has yet programmed a
computer to be of two minds about a hard problem or to burst
out laughing." But twenty years from now, when the class of
'80 is moving into senior positions in government, in industry,
and in the professions, computer technology will play an even
more fundamental role in social and economic analysis than it
does today. The ability of our graduates to make vital social
and business decisions will be seriously impaired if they do
not understand the possibilities and the limitations of this
new technology. Worse, they will find themselves in the
clutches of "experts," too intimidated to dispute the wisdom
of the machine. A fairly rudimentary understanding of data
banks, programming, and information retrieval systems will
make it far less likely that educated men and women will, in
the future, be over-awed and cowed into intellectual submis-
sion by mere printouts.

An expository writing requirement for freshmen, on the
other hand, does represent a neglected and traditional
"basic"—English composition, a requirement created to ensure that all students who receive a B.A. from our universities
can express themselves with clarity, precision, and even some
degree of grace. One does not necessarily have to believe in
the well-publicized culture of stupidity or in the dire import
of declining SAT scores to be in favor of reemphasizing writing skills in our undergraduate curriculum. It may well be
that SAT scores have fallen, as some maintain, not because
the traditional college-age population is less literate than

they used to be, but because the pool of those taking these tests has widened to include far more students from disadvantaged families, and others who ten or fifteen years ago would simply have not bothered with the testing programs that precede application to college. Or maybe the students of the 80s are just not good test-takers. It does not really matter why entering freshmen are, as a group, a shade less verbally dexterous than they were a decade ago. Certainly it does not mean that civilization as we know it is collapsing. What matters is that we as educators are according a new curricular primacy to the ability to write effectively. No elaborate justification for this is required.

I would argue that a man or woman who cannot speak and write clearly cannot think and reason cogently either. Psychologists tell us that human beings reason and analyze in words. Image-making and intuition may precede verbalizing, but we are not a preliterate society: we communicate with each other through the use of the spoken and written word. To barbarize and degrade the written language is to barbarize and degrade our thought processes and to damage our ability to reason together and to transcend superstitions, prejudice, and the use of force rather than intelligent and persuasive discourse.

Nor do I believe that there are those exceptional few—typically the top ten percent of a college's freshmen class—who should be exempt from a first-year course in expository writing. To do this is to penalize our most linguistically talented students, to say that it is precisely those with a real gift for written expression that should be denied the opportunity to hone their already superior skills to the point of utmost control and mastery. I do not take this view. An expository writing program must provide specially planned Honors sections for those who already write well. Why should they be denied a year to polish and develop a great gift? And why should the faculty forfeit the chance to work with the most promising and original student writers?

Those who enter college particularly blighted in their writing abilities may need to learn something as simple as how to craft the straightforward declaratory sentence. Those others who are far advanced in their command of English may use their year course to learn the devices of classical rhetoric, or they may devote themselves to mastering the literary polemic, the ironic or pathetic mode, the art of understatement or inference, or how to damn with faint praise. The latter, of course, will be particularly useful to future politicians and college presidents. Beyond simple proficiency, there are many levels of writing sophistication to which students can aspire.

My somewhat over-lengthy apologia for expository writing as a necessary ingredient of any general education curriculum should make it clear that I believe even courses that are nominally devoted to "the basics" should be so constructed as to encompass far more than mere remediation. Remediation of skills is frequently a necessary chore that a university must perform for some of its students. But by itself it does not get us very far, and if this were all that the new concern for general education signified it would indeed be a paltry effort.

I find myself generally unenthusiastic about the standard survey course that for many years was the principal way in which students satisfied distribution requirements. I refer to courses typically designated as *An Introduction* to Sociology, Psychology, Economics, or whatever. It seems to me that many of these courses, particularly in the social sciences where they abound, offer students neither depth nor breadth within their disciplines. One may argue that depth was never their goal, but breadth surely was, and yet the students that I have spoken to invariably seem to remember such courses as unsatisfactory hodge-podges—and dull to boot. One reason for this reaction is that such courses have usually been designed as starting points for concentrators—the first in sequence for the department's future majors. They were thus seen by the faculty as building blocks only and rarely thought of as coherent and vital entities in their own right.

If we are serious about general education for our undergraduates such an approach to the social sciences must change. In the first place, students must be taught to understand their interrelatedness. After all, whether it is economics or anthropology, social science deals with the complexities of human behavior, individually and in groups. Every student should have some conception of the different foci of the several disciplines that are collectively known as the social sciences; they are the branches of a single great tree; all (except, arguably, economics) have essentially developed within the last one hundred years; all have shaped our modern understanding of the world. It seems to me that it is not asking too much to expect college graduates to know something about the achievements of Freud *and* Weber, or Keynes *and* Leakey.

At the same time, teachers must convey some understanding of how social scientists gather and analyze their data and how social science differs from "hard" science at the practical as well as the theoretical level.

This may seem like a great deal, and we may have to construct some wholly new course offerings to attain these goals. Various attempts have already been made to teach the social sciences along less sectarian lines. It is possible, for instance, to teach a course on *The Family* utilizing economic, sociological, anthropological, and psychological perspectives. But rarely have such courses been designed to fulfill general education requirements. I see no good reason why this could not be done. Jealously guarded departmental prerogatives and suspicion of adjacent disciplines and crosslisted offerings have, I believe, been exaggerated. They are the great academic restrictions invoked by the timid to frighten off those with imagination and daring who believe that dynamic teaching and intellectual coherence are more urgent matters than strict preservation of departmental autonomy.

While I seem to be disparaging survey courses, let me turn to another: Western Civilization or History 1-2, the usually obligatory undergraduate monster course that begins somewhere in the Stone Age and ends with World War Two. That at least is what the college catalog announces. It cannot be denied that the intent of such a course is laudatory, even noble: it aims to give the callow undergraduate some appreciation and respect for the human community as it has evolved in the West over more than two thousand years. It is supposed to introduce students to the distinguished features of major historical epochs: the Middle Ages, the Renaissance, the Victorian Era. Ideally, students will come to understand something about the political order, the moral and aesthetic preoccupations, the scientific ethos, and the economic arrangements of society in each of these periods. They will at least recognize the great personage of history and will associate Louis the XIV with Versailles and Louis Napoleon with the Empire. No one who completes the course will henceforth be under the impression that Mussolini was an Italian painter.

Perhaps. But I am not convinced that this approach is the best that we can come up with. Given a rare charismatic lecturer supplemented by a small discussion group it may work. But we cannot always count on having inspired faculty members who are willing to take on such a load. And we should also recognize the limits of what we are imparting to our students with this very traditional pedagogy: the large lecture where students sit passive, and often dazed, while some academic eminence discourses learnedly on the rise of nation-states and the fall of kings is, in fact, a rather dated narrative chronicle of events that depends on conventional periodization, on military defeats and victories, and on great men.

This is not exactly an invalid way to teach students about the past. But in its way it is quite restrictive. There are sound reasons why historians consider the Spanish Armada and the Battle of Waterloo turning points. However, we should acknowledge that this kind of history tends to give short shrift to some of the most exciting work being done within the discipline today. A good many historians now view their subject as a social science; their concern is less with the deeds of kings and warriors than with the parameters of life as it was lived by ordinary, and therefore historically anonymous, men and women. There are historians today who are concerned with fertility and mortality rates, with the growth of cities, with changing crime rates, and, more recently, with the availabil-

ity of energy sources. Granted that all undergraduates should
have some exposure to historical subject matter, can we not
envision some alternatives to the blockbuster Western Civilization offering?

Lately, I have become intrigued by the possibility of
teaching history through literature and film. Such an approach that would familiarize students with the medieval
world through *Beowulf* and *The Little Flowers of St. Francis*
and through such films as *The Seventh Seal* is admittedly *not*
traditional. It is, on the contrary, highly innovative and perhaps a bit risky. But to me it is an approach that makes sense
if our goal includes introducing our students to the modes of
thought and the imaginative re-creations of other times. It is
folly to think we can ever recapture and arrest the whole of a
past culture; perhaps we would do better by being deliber-
ately selective, by giving students access to an experiential
dimension. By making explicit the subjective element in how
we view the past, we can at least disabuse them of the notion
that when they have taken a single course and read a few articles on, say, the French Revolution, they have exhausted all
there is to know about that subject.

While I am discussing unorthodox educational experiences, let me digress briefly to take note of a college whose
entire curriculum is—given the temper of the times—quix-
otic. I refer to St. John's College in Annapolis, Maryland, and
more recently also in Santa Fe, New Mexico. For over forty
years, St. John's has withstood all reformist pressures and
bucked all modernizing trends. Its entire undergraduate curriculum is prescribed. St. John's students—all of them—learn
the foundations of Western civilization by reading through
120 great books. The entire freshman year is devoted to the
ancient Greeks, and not until the senior year do students encounter such neophytes as Goethe and Darwin.

Paradoxically, this devotion to classical ideals makes St.
John's one of the most radical educational institutions in the
country today. In a world where humanists and generalists
perceive themselves as beleaguered on all sides by specialists
and subspecialists, St. John's continues to thrive. And I think

that is because it stands for something: the timeless liberal arts ideal of the wise man who pursues truth for its own sake. The utilitarian value of all this is perhaps nil. It is an inherently compelling vision or it is not. But it may well be the basis for sound thought, the ability to reason, and the foundation of effective communications.

While I am not advocating such a curriculum for everyone, I believe it is immensely valuable that it exists *somewhere*. What I admire most about St. John's is its sense of its own distinct identity. It ought to embolden faculties in other schools not to necessarily replicate the unique St. John's curriculum but rather to seek and create their own distinct identities. Educational pluralism is of vital concern to all. So too are educational standards—we need to know that a B.A. signifies some measure of knowledge and excellence. I do not believe that the two are incompatible.

A curricular question to which I see no easy answer concerns the role of non-Western cultures within general education. On the one hand it is undeniable that we are Westerners, the inheritors of a distinct Judeo-Christian cultural tradition that carries within it certain assumptions about man's nature, free will, ethical conduct, individual freedom, and human rights. Though a few years ago young people were flocking to Buddhist monasteries and incanting Indian prayers, I think we must all acknowledge that the Western tradition has shaped us, that it has inculcated us all with certain linear assumptions about progress and has given us all a certain confidence in technology. Clearly, college is the place—and the undergraduate years are the time—when young men and women should be exploring some of the philosophical, scientific, and legal assumptions of their cultural heritage.

But it is difficult to do this without at the same time succumbing to the illusion that our way—our political system, our notions about the purpose of society and the importance of personal happiness—is the best and, indeed, the only way. In a word, it is hard to escape our own cultural provincialism, which frequently becomes outright myopia.

Recently, after observing the jolting events of Iran's Islamic revolution, one of our more astute journalists, Meg Greenfield, remarked that, to use her words "we keep trying to fit their behavior to our models" thus betraying our implicit assumption that Islamic people are simply and obstinately "backward Westerners, Indo-Europe's slow learners."

And, although for different reasons, I think the same fault exists when we try to analyze the actions of the Soviet Union, and their response to our actions, in the frame of mind of Westerners. We must understand the world does not think in English, nor act in the American mold. Indeed, general education models must not exclude all mention of philosophical and cultural systems different from our own. We must begin to acknowledge, viscerally and emotionally as well as intellectually, that civilized society did not originate with Greece and Rome; in China, India, and in the Near East other models prevailed.

It seems to me critical that any general education component at least introduce students to cultures based on quite different value systems. There is no single prescribed way to do this. In the first place, there will be many academic institutions, generally the smaller ones, that will not have the faculty necessary to teach meaningful courses in, for example, Oriental philosophy or Japanese industrial development. Yet a way must be found. Since we cannot hope to give undergraduates—except perhaps those who elect to major in foreign studies—anything like a thorough understanding of a non-Western society, perhaps the best we can do is ask the student to select among a fairly wide range of humanities offerings in non-Western culture. Thus an art history major might elect Japanese landscape painting or a religion major choose a course on Buddhism.

I am not, however, wholly satisfied with this solution; for one thing I feel that it neglects social structures in favor of some aspect of culture that is, if not peripheral, then at least less difficult to apprehend. For another, humanities courses tend to present Asian and Near Eastern societies in their pristine age-old forms. The contemporary edge is missing, as is a sense of upheaval and change. Before the great non-Western cultures can be fully and adequately represented in our undergraduate curricula, I am afraid that a national commitment will have to be made to decreasing our Eurocentric view of the world. This charge—that we were running our colleges as though civilization began and ended with European man—was one that was frequently made in the 1960s, and although it led, given the temper of the times, to a lot of curricular nonsense, it also contained considerable truth.

However, giving students curricular access to another culture—and so much the better if this can be supplemented with a year or a semester of study abroad—is not at all the same thing as ethnicizing the curriculum. My opposition to this trend is fundamental. To teach Italian studies to Italian-Americans and Puerto Rican studies to those of Puerto Rican parentage may be immediately gratifying, and spuriously "relevant." But I believe that if we allow such programs to be substituted for the great literary, philosophical, and social science traditions of the West, we are cheating them blind. Yet, there are respectable academic institutions that have installed such programs. I believe that the student who devotes the time that should be spent on general education to this or any other academic byway is simply confirming and perpetuating his own parochialism.

Only if such programs can be constructed to achieve rigor, including a high level of foreign language proficiency, can they be said to be legitimate undergraduate pursuits at all. They should never be substituted for core curriculum experiences of the sort that bring students together in intellectually challenging and enlarging discourse. We have heard a great deal in the last decade about the diversity of our multiethnic student bodies, about their highly special and individual needs. Let us not forget that as 18 year-olds living in America of the 1980s, they have many common characteristics as well. One of them, surely, is a shared need to become acquainted with the great achievements of literature, art, and science in which we all have a stake.

Just as I am convinced that all undergraduates should

have their intellectual horizons broadened by study of another culture, quite distinct from our own, so too I believe we need to reemphasize foreign language skills. During the last decade, foreign language requirements were dropped by many schools and it is not difficult to understand why this happened. It is both expensive and time-consuming to teach students the grammar, syntax, and pronunciation of another language. And college, it seems, is not the optimal time to do it. If the development psychologists are to be believed, foreign languages are best learned before the age of nine. After that it becomes much more difficult and takes much longer. From the university's point of view, teaching foreign languages to beginners is anything but cost efficient. And even if a large commitment in time and money is made, too many students come away from this experience speaking French or German or Italian atrociously. Is it worth it?

Personally, I believe it is, but I also think that universities must find a way to promote foreign language study at the secondary and, especially, the primary school level. In the case of a large metropolitan university this might even mean special after school foreign languages classes for—at the very least—neighborhood children. If they can take violin classes or piano lessons twice a week, then why not Spanish or Russian? For the great majority who are not budding Heifitzes or Cliburns, language training would be far more useful.

Another point about languages: I read recently that for every college student currently studying Japanese in the United States there are more than a hundred studying French. Certainly, the magnificence of French literary achievements and the overall part that French culture has played in shaping what we call "civilization" will ensure the continued vitality of the French language in our university curricula. But the non-Western languages—Japanese, Arabic, Russian, and Chinese most conspicuously—must in the future receive greater emphasis. These languages represent the peoples who will be increasingly important in the world community in decades to come. We should prepare our students now, through language mastery, which is indispensable to acculturation. Language is the key to the social and psychological identity of another culture. If we do not understand Japanese or Arabic, we have small hope of understanding the Japanese or the Arabic peoples, and any judgments we make about their societies and their institutions will continue to be superficial.

The difficulties of finding a satisfactory way to build foreign languages into our curricula (redoubled in the case of languages that do not use Roman script) are exceeded only by the unanswered questions about how to teach natural science. The sciences are notoriously hard to teach and, except for the squadrons of aspiring premeds, undergraduates tend to be resistant to them. Those who worry about gradepoint averages feel that taking physics will jeopardize their chances of making the Dean's List. Many others report that their high school encounters with the "hard" sciences were so desultory that they have no inclination to risk a repeat experience. Regrettably, professors too sometimes despair of conveying any meaningful scientific knowledge to undergraduates whose academic interests lie in the humanities, preferring to devote their teaching efforts to declared concentrators in chemistry, physics, or biology or to the premed students.

By contrast, our need, as a society and as individuals, to be scientifically better informed becomes daily more urgent. The nuclear accident at Three Mile Island, and the ensuing debate, gave dismaying proof of the public's ignorance, and hence its extreme vulnerability when issues of scientific policy arise, as they increasingly will. Not only were people confused about the severity of the immediate crisis—this was perhaps unavoidable in view of the conflicting assessments of nuclear experts themselves—but abruptly all the myriad and enormously complex issues of radiation, its long- and short-term impact on water supplies, crops, and milk, the siting of nuclear power plants, and above all the trade-offs between potential nuclear problems and national energy needs were thrown into the hopper and became subjects of heated, not to say hysterical, controversy. The spectrum of opinion exhibited in the media stretched all the way from the *China Syn-*

drome afficionados who predicted that doomsday was at hand to those who discounted the whole Three Mile Island affair as a "hoax." Lacking even a basic understanding of most of the issues involved, the public was left suspicious, frightened, and antagonistic. Seldom has the need to raise our collective level of scientific literacy been more dramatically illustrated.

With each passing year, it seems that social and ethical issues that scientific advance forces us to confront become more numerous. Though many people probably do not know it, we are living in the midst of biological revolution. Since the discovery of DNA, our knowledge of the chemical basis of life has been transformed. Once again theories of the origin and evolution of life may soon be turned upside down. Our new knowledge of cellular structures already permits genetic manipulation: we will soon have the power to create relatively complex new organisms. This kind of research has the potential to bring enormous benefits to mankind. It is also filled with hazards. DNA, like nuclear energy, has become something of a public controversy. It is the responsibility of educators to see that our students are knowledgeable about this vastly exciting scientific frontier. The debates it has engendered will not, must not, be confined to professional scientists. We must see to it that our students have an informed basis for the judgments they will quite possibly have to make in town meetings and referendums.

In order to understand the topical and politicized scientific controversies now going on in our country, students must also understand something about the way scientists work, the nature of scientific proofs and paradigms, and the evolution of scientific thought. This is not an easy subject either to undergraduates or to older pupils, like myself, whose interests lie primarily in the humanities or the social sciences. Students must understand that both Newton and Einstein were the creators of models of reality that encompassed far more than physics. And finally, they must be prepared to think about the moral issues that underlie the social management of science.

How do we do all this? It should be painfully obvious that simply requiring a student to take the traditional laboratory science wherein he prepares noxious H_2S or breeds fruit flies does not accomplish very much. The science faculties at many universities have specifically recommended *against* this once mandatory episode in undergraduate education. It can be both painful and totally unproductive—Thurber's disastrous encounter with botany comes to mind.

Scientists, on the other hand, strongly believe in disciplinary training and the experimental method. They argue that in the natural sciences knowledge is organized vertically: you cannot plug in just anywhere, as is frequently possible when teaching history or literature. Asserting that disciplinary comes before interdisciplinary, scientists nevertheless are the first to admit that a way must be found to familiarize students with the major scientific discoveries and issues of the day. We must consider how best to do this, whether by creating special advance-level seminars on science and society, by requiring freshmen and sophomores to take some wide-gauge "foundations courses" that emphasize disciplinary epistemology, or simply by stiffening natural science requirements for all.

The problem of how to teach the natural sciences, and most especially their social dimensions, highlight one of my major concerns about undergraduate education. In undergraduate academic life, what most often seems to get squeezed out is the broadly integrative or synthesizing educational experience. Everyone agrees, at least in principle, that such experiences are absolutely vital. But the claims of preprofessional concentrations or "majors," of skills requirements, and of electives (that enshrine "freedom of choice") must also be respected. We must devise new ways to accommodate all these competing demands.

The need for synoptic or integrative education becomes even clearer when we consider that an increasing number of issues fundamental to the way we live do not fit readily under existing disciplinary or department rubrics. Let us once again consider energy resources, now on everyone's mind. The subject has obvious, albeit neglected, historical importance. The Industrial Revolution, which revolutionized the social order and the nature of work and family life, began with a revolution in energy production: Watt's steam locomotive and the internal combustion engine depended on the harnessing of coal as a new source of power.

For the next two hundred years, industrial and economic progress worldwide has been inseparable from energy resources. Thus, it seems to me odd that energy has never been treated as a topic for historians. It gets a great deal of attention from physicists, from environmentalists, and from economists. But it seems blatantly apparent that the subject is so vast, so important, and so multifaceted that it demands a cross-disciplinary perspective. To understand its full ramifications, we must understand not only the scientific aspects of energy production and consumption but their social context as well. So far, it has been left to politicians, journalists, and science fiction writers to educate the public on the vital questions of energy costs, allocation, and the social implications of an energy-scarce world. I do not think we can afford to leave it in their hands alone.

There are other subjects as well that do not get taught because they do not fit our standard curricular divisions. Law, for instance, increasingly permeates every aspect of our lives. Novelists need to worry about contracts and copyrights; doctors about malpractice suits, universities about equal opportunity laws, and live-in lovers about common property and the possible revival by the judiciary of updated breach of promise suits. Recently civil rights activists have mounted a drive to extend constitutional guarantees to groups of persons who traditionally have been excluded from various kinds of constitutional protection: incarcerated criminals, members of the armed forces, and children.

Yet, there is little if any reflection of this increased societal preoccupation with the law in our undergraduate curricula. At most universities, except for the one obligatory course on constitutional law, which generally concentrates heavily on eighteenth- and nineteenth-century Supreme Court decisions, the teaching of law is confined exclusively to law schools. To paraphrase Clemenceau, law is too serious a mat-

ter to be left to the lawyers. Philosophers, sociologists, and
historians need to be convened to explicate its deeper mean-
ings to our students. Whether they eventually become mathe-
maticians or musicians, they will be better equipped to understand the society they live in.

If we stop to think about it, the range of subjects that
seem to require cross-fertilization from two or more disciplines is potentially very wide. One of the foundations
courses at Middlebury is entitled Human Conflict—a subject that takes in individual frustration and aggression, 'racial and religious strife, and, as its most virulent expression,
war between nations. At Middlebury it is being taught from
the combined perspectives of history, political science, social
psychology and sociology—a distinctive and imaginative undertaking.

Boston University, another one of the schools that has recently made fundamental revisions in its curriculum, offers an
interdisciplinary course devoted to the study of New England
through history, literature, and the visual arts, focusing on the
changing conception of the New England identity.

At New York University we are on the verge of carrying
this interdisciplinary, integrated approach to learning several
steps beyond the discrete single semester course. It is an exciting project, and while we have some trepidations, we are
determined to take the plunge. The idea is a simple one: a
relatively small group of undergraduates, approximately 200,
will commit themselves to three full semesters of organized
study built around a seminal topic, one that includes dimensions that properly belong to the humanities, the social sciences, the arts and the natural sciences. Urban culture is such
a topic. Clearly, it lends itself to sociological and ethnological
perspectives. The city, ancient and modern, ideal and actual,
has generated an enormous amount of literature—consider
Augustine's *The City of God,* Lewis Mumford's *The City in
History,* and Hugo's *Les Miserables* to name but a few books.
Architects, urban planners, and filmmakers have all constructed visions of the city. Biologists as well as psychologists
have studied urban populations, crowds, mobility patterns,

and the social composition of neighborhoods. It is a vast, engaging, and supremely "relevant" topic even if one's home base does not happen to be New York City. The educational experience, which we are developing, is one that aims to involve the students fully. It will be designed to encompass a variety of learning and teaching modes: traditional lectures, "team teaching," collaborative research projects by small groups of students, etc. Guest speakers, who embody various kinds of urban expertise will be invited; films will be shown. We believe that this kind of structure will ensure that students acquire far more than a superficial pastiche of urban images and lore.

Other topics invite such cross-disciplinary studies and dynamic pedagogies. The faculty at New York University is developing several such integrated sequences. We do not expect our model to solve all our curricular problems; it may not even be appropriate for all NYU students. A significant portion of the faculty, I believe, finds it a bit educationally risque. But without such bold experiments, higher education in our country is in danger of becoming static or even regressive. And that would be nothing less than a social calamity that would ensure a dwindling of talent and human resources at a time in history when we need all the intellectual courage and daring we can muster.

Finally, what we demand of higher education, should also be demanded in the employment sectors of our economy. Certainly the Chief Executive Officers would hardly endorse these requirements. Why, I ask, are the recruiters who visit our campus so single minded in their pursuit for the vocationally trained.

We as educators have a great deal to do in our colleges and universities. We also have a great deal to do in the corporate sector. We must not teach to the transitory interest of the recruiters or students—but we must also do our best to explain why.

That may be our most difficult challenge. But if we are to succeed beyond the era of retrenchment, we must reach out as well as in. And we must succeed.

EDUCATION IN THE '80s[1]

David C. Knapp[2]

It has become almost ritual every ten years for pundits, scribes, seers, and others to attempt to characterize the departing decade and to prophesy what to expect in the coming ten years. Thus, it was not surprising after January 1, 1980, to hear speakers in various fields trying to capture the essence of the '70s and to predict the '80s. David C. Knapp, President of the University of Massachusetts, presented just such a speech on the future of education on February 11, 1980.

Disclaiming credentials as a soothsayer or futurist in the first sentence of his speech, President Knapp nevertheless sought to foresee the future of American higher education in the eighties. His central thought was: "The well-being of colleges and universities in the years ahead will depend on how we address at least four fundamental issues of academic policy." These issues, he indicated, were the result of changes in the majority-minority ethnic composition of college enrollments, the increasing number of students who will study while working, resolution of the debate on the relative values of a professional and a liberal education, and how to cope with a growing faculty malaise.

Of particular interest to college educators and administrators was his discussion of the issue of a liberal versus a professionally oriented education. "Unlike many of my colleagues, I cannot deplore the contemporary student's interest in earning a future living," he said, "I had such an interest myself." After expressing his opinion that liberal and professional education are not antithetic, Knapp suggested that,

> The real task which confronts us is to define the core intellectual experience which any student, regardless of principal interest, should encounter in a university within the context of his or her time. In the phrase "core intellectual experience," I include not only the fields of knowledge to which all should be exposed, but the nature of the intellectual encounter itself.

[1] Delivered at the annual New England Regional Assembly of the College Board at 10 A.M., on February 11, 1980, at the Marriott Hotel in Newton, Massachusetts.
[2] For biographical note, see Appendix.

Put simply, adding up introductory courses in a variety of liberal and professional fields does not constitute a core curriculum.

Dr. Knapp delivered his address to approximately one hundred admissions officers at the annual New England Regional Assembly of the College Board at 10 A.M., on February 11, 1980, at a meeting in the Marriott Hotel in Newton, Massachusetts.

I begin my remarks with a disclaimer on my credentials as a futurist. Thirty years ago, pursuing doctoral research at a desk in the Library of Congress, I had no idea that I was entering a decade which would witness the beginning of an unprecedented upsurge in public support for scientific inquiry and education beyond high school. Nor did I realize twenty years ago, while sitting in a library in Helsinki engaged in post-doctoral research, that the world of higher learning was about to become strife-torn, resulting in major changes in academic programs and governance. And, finally, as I sat at a dean's desk in Ithaca ten years ago, I foresaw neither the public disenchantment with higher education nor the fiscal crisis which would soon descend upon the academic world.

Change in higher education comes in ever shorter cycles, and much of what causes change lies outside the ken and the control of those responsible for academic life. Hence, if I have any single valid prediction to offer today, it is that higher education in 1989 will be influenced significantly by conditions and forces which none of us can now foresee, conditions substantially different from those upon which we base our current extrapolations.

With these caveats out of the way, let me now turn to the known. By all but those who remain stubbornly oblivious to demographic data, the decade of the 1980s must be seen as one of contraction, constraint, and competition. And unless the economic forces which have prevailed in the past seven years are reversed, the conditions flowing from demographic change will be exacerbated by oppressive rates of inflation.

I recognize that what I have just said is unpopular in many academic circles, that to accept the reality of smaller enrollments is seen as embarking on a path toward a self-fulfilling prophecy. Indeed, just recently, pages of the *Chronicle of Higher Education* were replete with quotations to this effect. The reasons for such reactions are readily understood. The majority of us who populate academia came of age professionally in the era of growth, reward, and respect. We find it difficult to believe that it ever was or ever should be otherwise. But the past was hardly as glorious as we sometimes imagine, and the future is already well-defined.

If we wish a better life, then we can hardly afford to equate quality with growth and size. We can no longer insist that an academic world shaped by the forces of the past is the only world in which higher learning can be pursued. Rather, we must get on with the task of dealing adequately with what we know the future holds.

The well-being of colleges and universities in the years ahead will depend on how we address at least four fundamental issues of academic policy. The list I outline today does not include the major organizational question: that of how we contract, institution by institution, or system by system. I do not address the issue simply because it has already received ample attention, but perhaps one additional comment is in order.

I have concluded that unless public policy is shaped carefully in the next several years, contraction will inevitably be felt most severely by the public and private institutions which responded most actively to the challenge of growth, which expanded—in the public interest—to educate an ever-larger number and growing diversity of young people. There is, of course, something patently unjust when those who responded to social challenge in one period are penalized for it in another. But beyond the fate of individual institutions looms a larger and more important question of social policy, whether such contraction will erode seriously the equality and the diversity of educational opportunity which has come to characterize American higher education in the past two decades.

I turn now to four of the many issues which I believe will shape academic change in the decade of the 1980s:

First majorities and minorities. From the data available, it would appear that birth rates have not been changing uniformly throughout American society. The middle income families who have historically sent their children on to college are having far fewer children than those who have not. As a result, those who have been termed minorities—blacks, Spanish-surnamed persons, economically and culturally disadvantaged whites—will in some parts of the nation move inexorably closer to being the majority in the normal college-age population. Indeed, projections in one western state indicate that black and Spanish-surnamed youth will constitute one-half of the 18 to 21 year old group by the end of the decade. They will everywhere constitute a substantial part of the pool of both the college student and the labor force potential. The final report of the Carnegie Council anticipates that by the year 2,000, one quarter of all college students will be members of minority groups.

I would submit that despite significant changes over the past decade, American colleges and universities continue to regard the education of these so-called "minorities" in our population as something special or unique, an exercise in affirmative action or social justice, touched by a latter-day sense of noblesse oblige. I would submit further that in the decade ahead we must learn to think and behave differently, in the interest of both institutional and national survival.

When I suggested this in a speech recently, a member of the lay audience responded that I was proposing a lowering of standards, a response that I found both irritating in its condescension and frightening in its perspective on the relationship of higher education to society. If our society is to function well, our task must be to send forth people who have trained intelligence at the higest levels possible, regardless of their origins or backgrounds. It may well be that we must work harder, and differently, to teach those who do not come from the middle class white families who have been the main beneficiaries of higher learning for a generation or more. But we and society as a whole will suffer if that is not precisely what we do.

Second, learning while working. Historically, colleges and universities, in this nation and elsewhere, have been oriented toward post-adolescents, those whom I would term for the purposes of these remarks, "the idle young." Certainly, many, including myself, have worked while learning, but for most, the learning experience has been primary, and work a means to that end.

In the decade ahead, the center of academic gravity will move toward another kind of learner—the one who learns while working. Such individuals will fall into two broad groups: first, those in search of formal instruction, credit and non-credit, at a later stage of life—to make a career change possible, to find self-fulfillment, to keep current with the state-of-the-art in a chosen profession or vocation; and second, those in search of knowledge to understand, and to make informed social choices about, the complex society in which they live.

Older students have gained considerable allure as possible substitutes for the traditional young. In my judgment, the numbers will be smaller than many expect. But that is hardly the issue. Rather, the question is whether traditional, youth-oriented colleges and universities can make the serious accommodations necessary for those who *will* come to "learn while working."

To date, despite much rhetoric in the past decade, life-long learning, continuing education, and extension education lie at the fringes of colleges and universities. I would contend that the needs of the older student will not be truly served unless they are woven into the very fabric of academic institutions.

The adjustments required go to the heart of the academic process. For the first group, those interested in some form of structured learning, the necessary adjustments cut across the full spectrum of academic life—from the admissions process and counseling, through course structure, class scheduling in time and place, the assignment of faculty time, and the reward system for its use, to the ways in which institutions invest in and use contemporary telecommunications for teaching and learning. For the second group, the adjustments strike at basic academic values, a consideration of the degree to which issue-related knowledge, stockpiled on the campus, can and should be put into meaningful form for laymen, and transmitted to them in ways unfamiliar and uncomfortable to the traditional academic. Even more important is the question of whether we are ready to give as much value and reward to such professional activity as we do now to instructing the young in the classroom and communicating with our peers in journals and seminars.

Third, professional and liberal education. I fully expect the current debate on liberal, and professional education to continue well into the 1980s. It should, for few things are more important to institutional vitality, in an era of uncertainty, than studied reflection on basic purpose.

Unlike many of my colleagues, I cannot deplore the contemporary student's interest in earning a future living. I had such an interest myself, and if I had had the loan obligations of the contemporary student, I would indeed have been anxious about my future. I continue to believe, as Charles Kellogg and I wrote some fifteen years ago, that an undergraduate should leave a university with at least one immediately marketable skill (which may include that necessary for admission to graduate and professional education) together with the knowledge and intellectual capacities to set him or her on the road to intellectual and personal growth over a lifetime.

To my mind, much of the current dichotomous debate misses the true issue. Liberal and professional education are not antithetical. In our highly technological and organizational society, they should be complementary, with each informing the other. The student in the basic disciplines is not truly liberally educated unless he or she possesses, for example, an understanding of the role of technology in the world today, its benefits, its costs, and the mode of thought of those who employ it. Conversely, students in professional fields can hardly function well if they do not have an understanding of the human and cultural milieu in which they will practice, be they engineers, physicians, or accountants.

The real task which confronts us is to define the core intellectual experience which any student, regardless of principal interest, should encounter in a university within the context of his or her time. In the phrase "core intellectual experience," I include not only the fields of knowledge to which all should be exposed, but the nature of the intellectual encounter itself. Put simply, adding up introductory courses in a variety of liberal and professional fields does not constitute a core intellectual experience.

To my knowledge, only one institution, the University of Vermont, has recently sought to address the contemporary nature of liberal and professional education as a unitary issue. Perhaps at a time when there is too much to know, too much to be learned, and too much to forget, the prospect of lending unity to learning in a university is dim. But the object is indeed worth the effort.

As we enter the twilight years of the 20th century, the basic ideas and values we debate differ little from those which preoccupied our predecessors at the century's beginning. But their context *has* changed. As one reads Robert Wohl's *The Generation of 1914,* one cannot help but be struck by how the pace of social change has quickened in the recent past. If a university education is to have value, current and future, if those who possess it, regardless of subject matter interest, are to give leadership to and live well in society, then we in our institutions must seek anew to help successive generations understand both the timeless and the timely in ever-shifting patterns.

Fourth, faculty malaise and intellectual vitality. The academic profession, after a fifteen-year night on the town, is experiencing a prolonged morning after. It is a damnably depressing time and the academic equivalents of aspirin and bloody marys are in short supply.

Depressed faculty morale ranks alongside inflation and demographic change at the top of the laundry list of problems with which we must cope as we enter the 80s. The academic profession is hardly as attractive as it once was. Salaries lag behind both price inflation and increases in disposable income outside the halls of ivy. External funding and internal support money are hard to come by and bureaucracy, self and externally engendered, grows in leaps and bounds.

As serious as the plight of the individual caught up in the current situation might be, it is the second order effects of depressed morale which should concern us most. An institution peopled by individuals concerned about personal security, self-esteem, and internal procedures soon loses its vigor as a center of intellectual life. It is also a poor place to get an education. And as the malaise spreads, the academic profession inevitably loses its capacity to attract the best and the brightest to replenish the nation's intellectual capital.

The seriousness of the problem which flows from faculty malaise is not, I believe, well understood. Our nation, our world is built on a foundation of knowledge and trained manpower, and that foundation is very fragile indeed. Knowledge rapidly becomes obsolete—unless it is renewed; the pool of manpower becomes useless—unless those already in the pool continuously refresh their training and newly trained individuals are added. The pace of change is increasing. The revolution in the biological sciences is just beginning; the social sciences give signs of emerging from their recent lethargy, as people like Rawls and Nozick and Bronfenbrenner challenge old concepts; past breakthroughs in the physical sciences are still giving rise to new applications; microprocessors are revolutionizing almost every aspect of human activity.

Ferment exists throughout the intellectual scene at the very time that our faculties are losing heart and turning inward. Unfortunately, if the latter spirit prevails, our universities may well lose their traditional role as the principal source of new knowledge and trained manpower and that spells disaster not only for us but for society as well.

We must break out of the dilemma. To this end, we can no longer look to the outside for help, any more than we can expect additional funds to bring about the needed internal changes. Rather we must demonstrate our own capacity to engage in self-help, to bring about—ourselves—adaptation to new times by redirecting activities and reallocating resources. Only then can we—and I believe we can—count on the generous support we have had in the past. Among those who would provide this help—parents as well as business and governmental leadership—there exists a deep-seated sense that during our long night on the town, we have become flabby and indecisive. Like the wife who stayed home, our traditional supporters are not sympathetic on the morning after. We must regain their confidence.

Wallowing in one's own misery seldom evokes sympathy or support. Willingness to address the problems of the time does. If we are willing to face squarely some of the issues I have noted here, if we are willing to upset the present equilibrium, to rearrange the chips on the board to ensure future academic vitality; if we are willing to pursue a different course in different times, then I believe we can engage the public's interest once again. Some faculty morale may suffer more in the short run, but over the long haul, I believe that we will emerge with a new sense of purpose and a refreshed sense of self-esteem.

I close with two observations. First, individual colleges and universities will and must respond to the issues of the 80s differently. We can ill afford to lose our special identities to substitute homogeneity for diversity as we strive to survive under stress. Just as the ideal of the research university became the model for too many in the decades just past, so we run the danger of some new ideal, born out of adversity, becoming unduly pervasive in the years ahead.

Second, how we address the issues of the 80s is quite as important as the issues themselves. In many circles I find a growing belief that only through a more hierarchical, a more industrial model of organization can academic institutions survive the 80s. I disagree. The academic life of the western world has from the earliest rested on the principle of self-governance, and it is this quality which has kept it not only alive, but growing and vital.

Unfortunately, the academic community, rather than setting an example for the larger community, now mirrors the fragmentation of society at large, translating the democratic process into one which supports special group interests and sets aside the search for commonality of values. Self-governance in academic institutions must be more than the veto of proposals for change. If we are to emerge from our long winter of discontent with life and hope, all of us who make up the academic community must together engage ourselves with reality, risk uncertainties, and thereby lend certainty to our successors.

THE OUTLOOK FOR CIVIL LIBERTIES

THE NEW CIVILITY:
THE INCREASE IN DEFAMATION[1]

DAVID J. MAHONEY JR.[2]

The Anti-Defamation League of B'nai B'rith presented its annual Man of Achievement award to David J. Mahoney Jr. on January 16, 1980. The award is made to someone who exemplifies or has contributed to goals of society, which are to promote racial and religious harmony, to reduce discrimination, and to protect the civil rights of American citizens. This was not the first time that Mr. Mahoney, Chairman and Chief Executive Officer of Norton Simon Inc., has been recognized for his leadership. The Anti-Defamation League presented him with its Torch of Liberty award in 1970. The Congressional Medal of Honor Society, the United States Marines, the Girl Scouts of America, and the Sales Executive Club also honored him with awards in the previous ten years.

The occasion for the presentation of the award and Mahoney's acceptance speech was a huge banquet attended by 1,500 people in the grand ballroom of the Waldorf Astoria Hotel in New York City. The audience was made up of members of the Anti-Defamation League, representatives of various ethnic and religious groups, business executives, men and women. The evening began early with an hour-long reception in another room in the hotel. After dinner, at approximately 8:30 P.M. actor and entertainer Alan King, who served as master of ceremonies, introduced the guests on the dais and Philip E. Beeckman, who presented a bouquet of flowers to Mrs. Mahoney. King then introduced Nathan Perlmutter who gave the keynote address. It was not until nearly 9:30 P.M. that Edgar M. Bronfman presented the Man of Achievement award and Mahoney responded with "The New Civility: the Increase in Defamation."

---

[1] Delivered at a banquet of the Anti-Defamation League of B'nai B'rith, in the ballroom of the Waldorf Astoria Hotel in New York City at 9:30 P.M., on January 16, 1980.
[2] For biographical note, see Appendix.

In his address, Mahoney called attention to what he perceived to be a serious challenge to society and the league—a new kind of defamation. He organized his speech according to the problem-solution method of division. Defining the problem as a growing "epidemic of bitterness between more and more groups in our society," he emphasized this idea with specific examples of the many bitter conflicts between men and women, insiders and outsiders, the young and their parents, businessmen and special interest coalitions, government and the press, and other groups, even including smokers and non-smokers. After illustrating the pervasiveness of the problem, Mahoney attributed its cause to a widespread "desire to be equal coupled with a fear of being the same, . . . the urge to stay special while insisting nobody is special." He then offered his solution—to learn to recognize the many differences among Americans without developing prejudice—and suggested ways in which this goal could be realized. He concluded the address, appropriately, on an optimistic and uplifting note.

The battle against prejudice is far from over. I think all of you will agree with me that there is a lot of work that still has to be done. Tonight, I want to put a couple of challenges in front of you. I hope you will accept these challenges in a spirit that will help the ADL [Anti-Defamation League] address the needs of the eighties and beyond.

First, and perhaps in a lighter vein, I think you ought to take a hard look at your name. "League" is all right, but I think your scope goes well beyond "Anti-Defamation." The word means "opposition to slander," but you do far more than that. Moreover, "Anti" puts it in a negative form whereas you have always been so positive. The negative might have been good in 1913, but in this day and age, people perhaps are more interested in what you are for than what you are against.

Second, a much more serious challenge that I would hope to see this organization take a lead in calling attention to is a new defamation: that epidemic of bitterness between more and more groups in our society.

In the old days, prejudice and bigotry basically applied only to racial and religious discrimination. The "KKK" by their definition stood for "Koons, Kikes, and Katholics." The main hatreds and tensions were between Gentile and Jew, WASP and Catholic, black and white.

Thanks to your work, to the work of the NAACP, The Urban League, the courts, and ultimately the American conscience, the old defamation, to a great degree but not enough, has been discredited and diminished.

But a new defamation, a new bitterness, has exploded. Spurred by a sharp increase in tension, there is a rising shrillness of rhetoric between those many groups fighting for equality, yet fearful of the equality they are striving to achieve.

Take a trivial example. On a shuttle flight between Washington and New York, a non-smoker demanded that the nonsmoking section be expanded to accommodate him, as the rules call for. The smokers sitting next to him refused. They started hollering at each other. The pilot, after his warnings to calm down were ignored, landed the plane not in Washington, not in New York, but in Baltimore. I think this is symbolic of what is going on in our society.

Consider a new form of disunity in our politics. The traditional battles between Democrats and Republicans, between liberals and conservatives. This is a fine and healthy thing. There has always been a conflict between the "Ins" and the "Outs" and a normal changing of the guard. But now there is a new edge of bitterness between the "Insiders" and the "Outsiders." I am speaking of the hints that candidates make when they "run against Washington." They characterize the insiders as a pack of fools or a center of corruption. The insiders lash back by contemptuously calling outsiders simpletons incapable of governing, irresponsible. You can feel that new bitterness.

What accounts for that new bitterness? Distrust of the outsiders is nothing new. I was sitting on a commuter train some time ago in one of those double seats that face each other with two men I had never met. We never said a word to each other as the train chugged along for ten or fifteen minutes. But when the train stopped, a fourth man joined us. The three of us looked at him. All of a sudden he was an outsider. And outsiders, to all of us, are threats.

Another area of defamation, new to our times, is the defamation between men and women. A new term has been added to our vocabulary: male chauvinist pig. What used to be called "manly" is now derided as "Macho," and the bitterness between the two groups goes both ways. I know one man who grimly insists that E.R.A. should stand for "Enough Rights Already." In our times, a simple chair has changed from something you sit in to something you talk to. In the minds of many Americans, the legitimate interest in achieving equal status for women has stirred a new tension—and a bitterness—between the sexes. The struggle on both sides seems not for fulfillment but for supremacy.

Consider, too, the new conflicts between the generations. Our young people demonstrated fiercely in the sixties. Since the seventies, they have withdrawn. They do not want to rebel so much as they want to disaffiliate. Many youngsters are disenchanted with the political leadership and turned off by parents who want only to be buddies and offer no guidance. As a result, with nothing to rebel against, they have turned inward past individualism into isolation. This is not as noisy a form of defamation, but it is even harder to handle.

Take defamation in business. Time was, labor and management would rail at each other as they wrestled for some economic advantage. But underlying that was a realization that they were in business together. Today, a new breed of anti-business idealogues, who find their ideas reflected by some government regulators, are engaged in a war on prosperity in the name of democracy. Businessmen no longer talk to customers or public servants. They talk to hard-eyed coalitions which are convinced that all profits are "obscene" and corporate America is, in their minds, motivated only by unbridled greed. Business is fighting back because we believe in the market system. My point is that a new form of business defamation is in the air.

And look at the way the government and the press are going at each other. Nobody in government calls the press the press anymore—they are "the media," a more sinister word that hints at manipulation and hidden persuasion. The courts have been issuing gag orders and in general trying to curtail the power of the press. Meanwhile, the press, or the media, often treats the government official as fair game for all forms and types of vilification. Sometimes the mutual complaints are true, but there is no reason for the intensity of the tension between groups.

I have not even touched on the resentment between the unemployed Americans and the illegal aliens, between the gays and the straights, between children drawn to cults and their parents, between the blacks and the Jews.

What is the cause of this explosion of defamation between groups? An obvious answer is economic—the have nots want what the haves have. But I do not think the obvious answer is the real answer. I think that a common denominator exists in almost all of these tensions. Once we recognize that key, we can unlock the problem.

The dilemma is this: As we all strive for equality, we all worry about what will happen to our uniqueness if and when we get equality. We want desperately to be equal, but we do not want to be the same as everyone else.

"Equality" is the name of the game. Whether it is women, or youth, or a racial or religious or ethnic group, that desire for equality is rightfully one of the driving forces of our times.

But so is "uniqueness." We all like to believe we are special, chosen, better in some way—that we have discovered a piece of truth that is superior in its uniqueness.

Indeed, we are often afraid of the very equality we seek. Prejudice, hateful as it is, is one thing we often revert to in order to help us preserve our identity. When barriers are broken down, as they should be, the fear of assimilation grows.

Young people want to be treated as adults, but they do not want to be adults. Women want the same rights as men, but they do not want to be the same as men. Members of individual religious groups want to be equal with other Americans, but they do not want to be the same as other Americans.

For the sake of argument, accept the idea I mentioned earlier that one of the basic causes of the increase in defamation throughout our society is this desire to be equal coupled with a fear of being the same. Put another way, it is the urge to stay special while insisting that nobody is special. We have to recognize these differences yet not develop prejudice.

If I am right—and I have run this idea past quite a few people who know a great deal more about psychology than I do—then if there is any truth at all to these subtle points, how do we reduce the level of defamation in our society? How do we achieve equality without sacrificing diversity?

Let us look at ourselves the way a marketing man looks at his market—segmented in a dozen different ways by age, sex, income, education, geography, and so on. As individuals, we are members of dozens of groups. I am a businessman and in my fifties. I am also a father, a Catholic, a football fan, and a smoker—except when taking the Washington shuttle. The interests of the different groups I belong to often conflict.

The recognition of our multiple associations should reduce the passion of our resentments. As we achieve equality, or enable others to achieve equality, we must remember the many different sources of our uniqueness. You do not have to be Irish to like corned beef and cabbage, or Jewish to like chicken soup.

There is another fundamental way to control the conflict between the thirst for equality and the hunger for uniqueness. It is to recognize the many sources of bitterness and defamation now spreading through our world and to consciously adopt a new civility.

A generation ago, Walter Lippmann said: "There is such a thing as the public philosophy of civility. It does not have to be discovered or invented . . . but it does have to be revised and renewed."

I do not see the new civility as any goody-goody excess of politeness. I see it as the willingness to avoid patronization, the willingness to extend respect for another's point of view—wrongheaded though it may appear—and demanding an equal respect for my own opinions, wrongheaded though they may seem to him or her.

The new civility demands a rejection of all stereotypes,

because it recognizes that everyone is unique and not just a stock character out of central casting.

The new civility recognizes the wisdom of editing our own remarks—to delete some of the expletives before they are spoken, to keep from impugning a group's motives before they have an opportunity to explain their point of view. This, it is to be hoped, will reduce the bitterness of debate. The old Lincoln story comes to mind of the man terrified during a thunderstorm: "O Lord, just a little more light and a little less noise."

It is time to apply some of that editing inherent in the new civility to my own remarks. Let me conclude with a parable that is part of the Jewish tradition.

The Bible tells us that, when Moses parted the Red Sea and led his people across to freedom, a prince of the tribe of Judah named Nashon was singled out for special honors. The Bible does not say why this particular prince was so honored, but tradition has it that when Moses told his people to wade into the Red Sea and that it would part for them, the people hung back. Only Nashon had the faith to wade in, and only when he was in up to his nostrils did the sea part, permitting the Israelites to escape.

I do not think it is too much to suggest that the seas of hostility and bitterness that we face today—in so many new relationships between groups—can be parted by people of good will. It requires faith, understanding of the fear of the consequences of equality and corresponding loss of uniqueness, self-confidence, and the willingness, like Nashon, to wade in.

Recently, an incisive writer observed that for whatever its ups and downs, its triumphs and its tragedies, this year, this decade must make us more aware that our hopes can not be realized by looking solely to ourselves but by looking outward, together. We are inexorably linked to each other.

The moments we have to share together are all too brief. It is in this spirit I gratefully accept your honor.

THE STATE OF CIVIL LIBERTIES[1]

CHARLES McC. MATHIAS JR.[2]

In the opinion of John Shattuck, Legislative Director of the American Civil Liberties Union, "The political upheaval which swept the country on election day" in November, 1980, created a "crisis of major proportions for civil liberties." According to Shattuck:

> Well organized and financed political action committees succeeded beyond their wildest dreams in driving out of office some of the staunchest supporters of civil liberties, wresting 12 Senate seats and majority control of the Senate from the Democrats and taking 33 previously Democratic seats in the House. What is important for us is not that those who were defeated were Democrats, but that their voting records on civil liberties issues were among the best in Congress. Already, those political action committees, heady with success, have targeted more than 20 other members of Congress, both Democratic and Republican, for defeat in 1982. Many of these also are among the best civil libertarians in Congress. (*Civil Liberties*, N. '80)

On January 25, 1981, Senator Charles McC. Mathias Jr. of Maryland, addressed the Anti-Defamation League of B'nai B'rith of San Jose, California, on the topic, "The State of Civil Liberties." He was principal speaker at a banquet of the civil rights organization which presented its Torch of Liberty for Distinguished Leadership to Gordon E. Moore. His audience consisted of approximately 300 people assembled in the California Ballroom of Marriott's Great American Hotel in San Jose. Following an introduction of guests and presentation of the award, Senator Mathias began his speech at approximately 8:30 P.M.

The *Almanac of American Politics, 1980* describes the Republican senior senator from Maryland as "a model of probity and integrity."

---

[1] Delivered to the Anti-Defamation League of B'nai B'rith of San Jose, California in the ballroom of Marriott's Great American Hotel in San Jose, at 8:30 P.M., on January 25, 1981.

[2] For biographical note, see Appendix.

Mathias is the old-fashioned kind of Republican for whom
one of the party's main attractions is its historic record on civil
rights; he was not pleased to see his party dominated by civil
rights foes such as Barry Goldwater. . . . He is one of those senators whose views are considered sound and whose judgment
on difficult issues is respected and sought. He is cautious, serious, not eager to take a stand; but when he does, he is listened
to. . . . He has high ratings from liberal and labor organizations. . . . In all, he seems a man more temperamentally suited
to the role of careful, judicious opposition than to strong advocacy of any establishment's program.

The senator is six feet tall, weighs about 180 pounds, and has
brown hair and blue eyes. His informal style and easygoing, confident manner have helped him win the respect of his constituents.
Former Senator Mike Mansfield said that Mathias is popular because "he doesn't go off on tangents, because he's not opinionated,
and because he's got a great sense of humor." (Washington *Post*,
Ag. 23, '71)

Other speeches by Senator Mathias appear in the 1972–1973,
1977–1978, and 1978–1979 volumes of *Representative American
Speeches*.

It is an honor to address the Anti-Defamation League of
San Jose and it is a great pleasure to be here to see you confer
the Torch of Liberty for Distinguished Leadership on Dr.
Gordon E. Moore of Intel Corporation.

Tonight, I want to talk a little about both leadership and
liberty in America today because I think we have some reason
for concern about them.

Five days ago we inaugurated the 40th president of the
United States with all the solemnity the occasion demands
and with all the hoopla and huzzahs it inspires. In Washington and on television screens across the land, bands marched
and people danced to the tune of "Thumbs Up America," a
song written especially for the occasion.

Everything about January 20 was upbeat. There was a
spirit of hope in the air; there was enthusiasm for "A New
Beginning."

But there were also some haunting, disquieting memories.
Four years earlier, America's hopes stirred to the populist ca-

dence of Jimmy Carter's feet as, hand-in-hand with Mrs. Carter, he led the inaugural parade on foot from Capitol Hill to the White House. That simple touch sparked the hope that, in President Carter, America had found a leader close to the people who would attend to their most basic needs—the need to find a job or to keep a job—the need to feed and clothe themselves—the need to heat their homes.

But, as inflation soared, those hopes were dashed. And the financially-beset American people proved on November 4, as the Book of Proverbs tells us, that, "hope deferred maketh the heart sick." They went to the polls and pulled the plug on Jimmy Carter.

Believe me, the gurgle was heard around the world. Right after the election I took a trip to Europe where people couldn't talk about anything else. Everywhere I went I got the same insistent, persistent question: "Has America turned fundamentally to the right?"

Meanwhile, back here in America, pollsters, pundits, politicians and just plain people were asking themselves, and each other, exactly the same question. And even now we're still trying to figure out how broad a mandate the American people have bestowed on Ronald Reagan.

I don't pretend to know the answer to that question. I have some ideas about it, but I don't think anyone can know the answer so soon. What troubles me—and I think it should trouble you too—is that some groups and individuals seem to have drawn a lesson from the election that it doesn't teach. There are disturbing signs on Capitol Hill, for example, that the election results have been taken as a license to declare open season on our civil liberties.

Personally, I think the only lesson this election teaches is that over four difficult years the American people became more and more apprehensive about the future. They pondered Ronald Reagan's simple question: "Are you better off now than you were four years ago?" And they gave their answer at the polls.

So, I don't think we need look any further than the failures of the Carter Administration to plumb the meaning of the election—inflation and unemployment, up; American prestige and power, down; leadership, non-existent.

Certainly, I can see no justification for construing the election results as an invitation to undo two decades of progress in assuring all Americans their civil rights and their civil liberties.

But, as a friend and as a fellow civil libertarian, I must warn you that in this election forces surfaced in our society that threaten our historic commitment to protecting minority rights. These forces will not soon, nor easily be laid to rest.

If you doubt the seriousness of my warning, ask yourself these questions:

Why should it take an hour-long conversation with Marc Tanenbaum to convince Jerry Falwell that God hears the prayers of Jews?

What does it portend for civil liberties when the Chairman of the Senate Judiciary Committee favors repealing the Voting Rights Act?

How comfortable can we feel about any of our civil rights achievements, if members of the Senate can use procedural tactics, including funding, with impunity to circumvent the legislative process?

Last spring, in the name of balancing the federal budget, Senator Helms introduced an amendment to cut the funds for the Civil Rights Commission in half. When a colleague remarked that it looked as if he were trying to kill the Commission, Senator Helms replied, "Right." Happily, that particular amendment failed.

But during the lameduck session of the Congress, the appropriations process was successfully breached when the Senate passed a bill amended to forbid the Justice Department from spending money on legal cases which involve busing to further school desegregation.

That action raises the red flag of danger above our liberties. It shows that now, without debate, without deliberation, simply by adding riders to appropriations bills, it is possible to gut the civil rights legislation we worked so hard to enact in the 1960s.

I do not maintain that our policy on school busing is immutable and sacrosanct. Indeed, I have argued for taking another look at how effective an instrument it has been in promoting desegregation and for creating a better alternative. But I do adamantly maintain that programs and policies adopted to promote equal justice in our society are not up for grabs. If changes are to be made in them, let them be made through the normal legislative process after careful deliberation, after hearings where all sides are aired and all shades of opinion are expressed. Or let them be made through the judicial process—but not through the backdoor—not by abusing the appropriations process.

The threat to our civil liberties is not an isolated phenomenon found only in the Senate. Danger flags dot the horizon from coast to coast. In May, the leader of the U.S. Nazi Party got 43 percent of the vote in the Republican Primary in North Carolina; a month later, as you well know, the Grand Dragon of the California Ku Klux Klan won the Democratic Primary in this State's 43rd Congressional District.

As usual, the Anti-Defamation League of B'nai B'rith has been quick to scent the danger. I am only sorry that the recent report of the ADL task force, convened to survey anti-Semitism in America, has received so little coverage in the press.

It found, as you know, that America is witnessing a revitalization of anti-Semitism that has been dormant for decades. In 1980, 377 anti-Semitic acts were reported compared to 129 in 1979. More than two-thirds of the incidents—which included swastikas smeared on synagogues, fire-bombings and anti-Jewish graffiti—occurred in the northeast.

It pains me that in my state, Maryland, the Ku Klux Klan is recruiting in the high schools and burning crosses on suburban lawns. In a recent interview with the *Washingtonian* magazine, the Imperial Wizard of the Klan, who lives outside of Baltimore, boasted of a guerilla war training area in Frederick County—the county where I was born and raised—and said they had a computerized enemies list and death squads. When asked who their enemies were, he replied: "Jew leaders—the B'nai B'rith and so forth, communist leaders, and the big niggers and race traitors."

When words like that can command any kind of an audience, it is time for decent men and women to speak out.

Last week, National Urban League President Vernon Jordan did speak out. He warned that racism:

is becoming legitimatized again and there is a direct link between the sophisticates who feel free to make derogatory remarks about blacks and other racial groups and the primitives who kill and terrorize. They are only separated by the degree of their activity.

Now, it is up to all our leaders to take a stand.

I don't mean to sound alarmist, but I think it is significant that political scientists recently have taken to comparing conditions and attitudes in the United States today with those that prevailed in the Weimar Republic in the 1920s, paving the way for the Nazi takeover.

Kevin Phillips in the November *Harper's* found these parallels:

. . . a middle class undercut by inflation, cultural malaise, military defeat, frustrated nationalism, loss of faith in institutions.

No one would deny, I think, that those conditions exist in the United States today. It is our job to see that they do not lead us down the road to disaster.

If we are to avoid the Weimar experience, we must take alarm at the slightest feint in the direction of our civil liberties. I believe it was Pastor Martin Niemoller who said:

When they came for the communists, I didn't speak out because I wasn't a communist. When they came for the Jews, I didn't speak out because I wasn't a Jew. When they came for the Catholics, I didn't speak out because I wasn't a Catholic. Finally, when they came for *me* there was no one left to speak out.

Let us not make the same mistake. Let us speak out now. Let us examine with microscopic care the Heritage Foundation report which warns that "the threat to the internal security of the republic is greater today than at any time since World War II."

Its recommendations include ending restrictions on mail

openings by the FBI and relaxing current safeguards governing FBI break-ins and wiretaps.

As a refugee from President Nixon's Enemies' List, I admit to a special sensitivity about relaxing those safeguards. And, as one of those targeted for defeat last year by the self-styled Moral Majority, I admit to a certain bias where that group is concerned.

But I believe those experiences also give me the right to speak as I am speaking to you tonight. Those who have been through the fire know best how to damp its flames.

In times of great change—and this is such a time—it is often useful to look at ourselves and our society through the eyes of an impartial witness. An astute British observer of America has written:

> Even if the Republicans should make a clean sweep, even if the State Department is cleaned out from the Secretary to the doorkeepers, even if the Pentagon is purged from the Joint Chiefs of Staff to the leaders of the rescue teams who find lost visitors, one problem of American policy will remain: the problem of the existence in the American mind, of what I call the illusion of omnipotence. . . .

> The idea that I am trying to describe is expressed by Senators and columnists, by candidates, by preachers, by people overheard in taverns and club cars, in drugstores and restaurants—the idea that the whole world, the great globe itself, can be moving in directions annoying or dangerous to the American people only because some elected or non-elected Americans are fools or knaves.

These are the observations of Dennis Brogan, longtime professor of political science at Cambridge and author of many books about the United States. They were intended as a warning to thoughtful Americans on the eve of the election of 1952. They are no less valid today.

The curtain then had just gone up on Senator Joseph R. McCarthy, who played the villain in a tragedy that rent and stained the fabric of American society.

Let us resolve together here and now not to become the audience for a revival of that sordid melodrama.

TO BUILD A MORE EQUAL SOCIETY: THE DUTY OF THE NEW ADMINISTRATION[1]

VERNON E. JORDAN JR.[2]

The election victory of Ronald Reagan and conservative Republican candidates at the polls in 1980 was perceived in some quarters as a setback for the aspirations and needs of blacks and other minority groups. The country's economic troubles seemed especially harsh on minorities and the poor, as unemployment rates rose and welfare payments lagged. Minority group leaders feared that resurging conservatism in Congress posed a threat to the hard-won Voting Rights Act, the food stamp program, fair housing, school busing, and other measures designed to aid the disadvantaged.

While most of the country switched from the Democratic side in 1976 to the Republican side in 1980, blacks in America remained faithful to the Democratic party, although in lesser numbers than before. In a speech to the National Urban League on November 20, 1980, Vernon E. Jordan Jr., its president, attempted to analyze the reasons for the change in leadership, to predict the implications of the conservative sweep for blacks and other minorities, and to chart a course of action for the future. Waldo W. Braden, editor of the 1979–1980 volume of this series, stated, "Without a doubt, the League's president, Vernon Jordan Jr., is the most articulate black spokesman in the country and he can exercise influence with the highest levels of the nation's leadership. As a public speaker, he is fluent and persuasive, ranking among the best on today's national scene."

Marian Christy, of the Los Angeles *Times,* described the 45-year old Jordan as "a very tall man [6 feet, 4 inches], a Hollywood-handsome hero with finely-chiseled features and a wide smile that alternately projects irony, majesty, or jest. His eyes are cool, calculating, appraising and the expression doesn't change to coordinate with the smile." "Everyone who knows Vernon Jordan knows that Vernon Jordan loves to talk," Christy added.

[1] Delivered at the National Urban League's Equal Opportunity Day awards banquet held in the New York Hilton Hotel, New York City, at approximately 9 P.M., on November 20, 1980.
[2] For a biographical note, see Appendix.

During the past decade, the National Urban League has emerged as one of the most important and smoothly run civil rights organizations. Its activities in behalf of blacks and its research reports on their status and progress receive wide attention.

Jordan's November 20, 1980, address took place at the League's Equal Opportunity Day dinner, an annual awards banquet, held in the New York Hilton Hotel. The speech was delivered around 9 P.M. to a diverse audience of approximately 2,000 League members and supporters, business executives, and media representatives.

Jordan's expression of thanks to officials of the League for their work "while I was out" and his introduction of "some of the people who helped save my life" referred to the assassination attempt in Fort Wayne, Indiana which hospitalized him for 98 days, less than six months earlier.

The National Urban League's Equal Opportunity Award honors outstanding Americans who have made significant contributions to equal opportunity.

Tonight's awardees—Irving S. Shapiro and Eleanor Holmes Norton—exemplify that tradition. Two dedicated people; one white, one black, one man, one woman, one representative of the private sector, one from the public sector—living examples of the diversity and interdependence of our society.

And although our selections for this year's EOD Award were made long before the election, they take on an important meaning today. They symbolize the National Urban League's belief that America's racial problems will not be solved without the total involvement of the private sector; and they reflect our belief that affirmative action is an essential element in the drive for equality.

While we of the Urban League movement thank Irving and Eleanor for their accomplishments and for allowing us to honor ourselves by honoring them, let me add a note of personal thanks to all those whose good wishes, kind thought, and fervent prayers helped me to recover from the attempt on my life last May.

And a note of very special thanks to John Jacob, Executive Vice President of the National Urban League, who did such a terrific job running the agency while I was out; and to the staff and volunteers of the entire movement. They demonstrated that we are indeed a movement and they provided services and advocacy without missing a beat during my absence. Thanks too, to my friends Dave Mahoney and Frank Thomas, who came to the hospital so often the staff there called them Dr. Mahoney and Dr. Thomas.

I'd like to introduce to you some of the people who helped save my life—Dr. Jeffrey Towles and Dr. Al Stovall from Fort Wayne, Dr. LaSalle Leffall of Howard University, and Doctors Adrian Edwards, Tom Shires, and Mike Yarborough of New York. They are all great doctors and, like everything else about the Urban League, they are an integrated team—black and white together.

A word of thanks too, to three ministers who helped heal my spirit—Dr. Howard Thurman, my pastor Reverend Simon Bowie, and Dr. Gardiner C. Taylor. And to all of you who showed concern and support for me, for my family, and for the Urban League—my heartfelt thanks. I also want to express appreciation to the New York Police Department and to the three officers who helped protect me—William Hubbard, Ken Mosby, and Al Sallie.

But we are not here to dwell on Fort Wayne and its aftermath. Fort Wayne is behind us. It is over. It is done with. It is well with my soul. I am recovered. I have no nightmares, no bitterness. I am not afraid.

In the words I learned as a little boy in Sunday School: "Forgetting those things which are behind and reaching toward those things which are before, I press toward the mark."

And that mark—for me personally and for the National Urban League—is the creation of a society in which black people and white people share equally in the rewards and responsibilities of our nation.

After November 4th, it is clear that our efforts to build a more equal society will take place in a political atmosphere that is markedly conservative.

It would be too simplistic to interpret the election results either as evidence of a massive swing to the right or as an overwhelming rejection of liberalism. Fifty-one percent of half the eligible voters is not the right wing mandate some observers have claimed.

People did not vote for or against political philosophies; they looked at the candidates and the nation; they saw high inflation and high unemployment and they did precisely what they did in 1976—they voted against the party in power. The only dissenters from that decision were the chief sufferers of both inflation and unemployment—black and Hispanic voters.

Why did the black vote stay in the Democratic column? Why were blacks almost alone on the deck of the sinking ship when others in the Democratic coalition were swimming to safety by switching to Reagan?

In part, the answer is that black voters did not perceive a Reagan candidacy as a safe harbor. What other Americans saw as a feasible alternative to failed leadership, most black voters perceived as the greater of two evils. And they did so despite deep dissatisfaction with the present administration. They feared the loss of important government programs that spell survival for millions of poor people. They did not believe in the promise that the private sector would end unemployment, because that has never happened.

Another part of the answer is that many black voters did *not* stick with the President—they stayed home rather than endorse economic policies that led to high black unemployment. And most black voters did what black voters always have done—they rewarded their friends; they voted for Carter and then switched party lines to vote for Republicans like Senator Mathias of Maryland.

Those of us who said the black vote would be crucial in this election were wrong, but only in a technical sense. The lesson of 1980 is that the black vote cannot make much of a difference in a landslide. But very few national elections are landslides. In a fairly close election black voters—potentially eleven percent of the electorate—will hold the balance of power.

That is something Republican Party strategists cannot ignore. We hear a lot these days about a permanent realignment in American politics; of a shift in the coalitions making up the parties and of a shift in political power to the Sunbelt.

But such sweeping generalizations will be proved true only if a Reagan presidency delivers on its promises of peace and prosperity for all and if, in the process, it succeeds in winning the loyalty of significant numbers of black voters. For it is that tenth of the electorate that will provide the winning margin in a close election. It is black and Hispanic voters who will hold the key to electoral victories in powerful Sunbelt states like California, Texas, and Florida.

So it would be a major political mistake for the Republican Party to assume, on the basis of the 1980 election, that it can ignore the black vote. And it would be equally serious a mistake for the Democratic Party to assume it can rebuild its shattered coalition while taking the black vote for granted.

If the Reagan Administration protects black social and civil rights gains, and if it fulfills its promises to wipe out unemployment, it can add blacks to its emerging new coalition.

It is far too early to make any predictions about a Reagan Administration's ability, or even its willingness, to meet the needs and aspirations of black Americans. I am hopeful that it will do so, in its own self-interest and in the nation's interest.

But black people cannot passively wait to see what happens. We must organize now to devise survival strategies for the next four years. Those strategies must be based on the political realities as they are, not as we wish them to be.

On one level, those strategies must be defensive. There are numerous federal programs that will come under heavy attack in the coming months. Like all presidents, Mr. Reagan will move toward the political center in order to govern. But the new Congress now has a disproportionate number of right-wingers. At this very moment they are sharpening their axes to cut and slash away at the basic interests of the poor, interests we must fight to defend.

Food stamps are in trouble. Affirmative action is in trouble. Education aid is in trouble. Fiscal aid to cities is in trouble. Welfare is in trouble. Public jobs programs are in trouble. Health assistance is in trouble. Civil rights laws are in trouble.

The list is as long as it is sad. We've got to start now to revitalize the coalitions that will be needed to defend the programs and principles black people and poor people depend on. There can be no compromising the vital interests of our constituents.

At the same time, we refuse to confine ourselves to a purely defensive posture; we refuse to accept four years of trench warfare to protect past successes without expanding to new territory and new victories.

But those efforts must be in tune with the realities of our time. We must adjust to those realities, just as a president who says he will cut taxes and spending while running in an arms race will ultimately have to confront reality.

Black people are not wed to any given political philosophy. Our needs are not bounded by liberal dogma. We are pragmatic. We want results, and if conservative means will move us closer to equality we will gladly use those conservative means.

We have a responsibility to come up with fresh ideas and new initiatives that help the poor and minority people who are our constituents, while recognizing the current conservative climate.

One such idea is welfare reform.

That may surprise many people. Welfare is supposed to be on everybody's hit list. But I believe that this is the time to fight for a complete, sweeping overhaul of the welfare system and its replacement by an income maintenance system that is in the best traditions of humane conservatism.

The liberal approach to welfare is often confined to larger allotments. The reactionary approach is to dump welfare programs on the states, converting a national problem into many local problems dealt with by hostile local bureaucrats.

But a truly conservative solution to the welfare problem would be one that puts cash directly into the hands of the poor, reduces the red tape and bureaucracy that has such arbitrary power over poor people, and gives to the poor the same freedom of choice and the same responsibilities enjoyed by others.

So a conservative solution to welfare points to the plan

the National Urban League has advanced—an income maintenance system based on the refundable income tax. Our plan would ensure that all people have minimum income levels and maximum freedom. It is a realistic alternative to the monster system that serves both the nation and poor people badly.

If the Reagan Administration backs the refundable income tax as a replacement for welfare and if it comes up with other conservative solutions to the pressing needs of poor people and black people, then it will demonstrate that conservatism with a human face has some of the answers we need.

I see some points of convergence. We of the Urban League know that racism and selfish opposition to minority advancement is fueled by fear; the fear middle Americans have of being sunk by inflation, lower real incomes, and unemployment. When the economic pie is growing, Americans proved willing to set another place at the table. Today, that pie is shrinking and we see black and poor people pushed away from the table.

Mr. Reagan says—with us—that the answer is to bake a bigger pie. Now, we want to hear him say—again, with us— that all Americans should have an equal opportunity to sit at the national table and enjoy their fair share of America's pie.

The president-elect is no stranger to the Urban League. In August he came to my bedside. He addressed our National Conference. He made some promises there. He promised "jobs, jobs, jobs." He promised never to fight America's problems on the backs of the poor. He promised his support for equal opportunity. He promised steps to create jobs in poverty areas.

We intend to hold him to those promises. We intend to take him at his word. We intend to work with his administration to help it succeed. America has only one president at a time and, as of January 20, like it or not, it is Ronald Reagan.

We have a responsibility to our president, our constituents, and our nation to fight for the rights and needs of black, minority, and poor people. We have the obligation to press forward with creative solutions to national problems. We have the duty to help educate the new administration to understand the interdependence of all Americans—an interdependence that is the lifeline of our pluralistic society and a mirror for an interdependent world.

So we must speak loud and clear to our president and to our nation with the message that the aspirations of black people in America's ghettos cannot be denied and that the aspirations of the black nations of Africa cannot be ignored.

We of the Urban League will never let the new administration forget Mr. Reagan's promises to us last August. We will never let it forget that black people too, are Americans; that like others, our blood, sweat, and tears built this nation, made it great, sustain it today, and will rebuild its greatness tomorrow.

We will let the new administration know that, like all Americans, we have a vested interest in its success. If a President Reagan puts America back to work again, black people will have to get those jobs too. If he cuts inflation, black dollars will go further too. If he keeps the peace, black lives will be saved too.

We are not liberals. We are not conservatives. We are Americans. We demand for ourselves what the white majority has always had—no more, no less. We look to our new national leadership with hope. We temporarily lay aside our fears and our misgivings. May we never have cause to bring them forward again.

Just about one week before the election, thirty Americans were sent back here from Cuba. One was a Black Panther who had hijacked a plane back in 1969. At that time he told the crew: "I would rather be in prison in Cuba than here." Now he is back. And what did he say? "The United States is the greatest country in the world. If the electric chair were waiting for me tomorrow, I'd return there."

America is indeed the greatest country in the world. And much of its greatness rests on its flexibility, its capacity for change. Black people know well that America can change. It can change because we have seen it change; we have made

America change. So as we confront a new administration and a new mood, the attitude of black people and the Urban League is summed up in a song that says:

> I don't feel no ways tired.
> I've come too far from where I started from,
> Nobody told me the road would be easy,
> I don't believe he brought me this far to leave me.

We know we will get over because we have the faith of our forebears, a faith that says: "Let justice roll down as the waters and righteousness as a mighty stream."

We have the faith of our forebears, a faith that makes us look toward the day when:

Every valley shall be exalted, and every mountain and hill shall be made low: and the crooked shall be made straight, and the rough places plain. And the glory of the Lord shall be revealed, and all flesh shall see it together for the mouth of the Lord hath spoke it.

Armed with that faith in the future and with our unshake-able thirst for equality, we face the future unbowed, un-moved, and unafraid.

APPENDIX

BIOGRAPHICAL NOTES

ANDERSON, WILLIAM S. (1919–   ). Born, Hankow, China; educated, public and Thomas Hanbury schools, Shanghai; internal auditor, Hongkong & Shanghai Hotels Ltd., 1938–39; auditor, Linstead and Davis, 1940–41; National Cash Register Company (now NCR Corporation), 1945–   ; manager, Hong Kong, 1946–59; vice-president for Far East and chairman, National Cash Register, Japan, 1959–72; Corporate President and Director of NCR, 1974; Chairman of the Board, 1976–   ; affiliations, Advisory Council on Japan-United States Economic Relations, ASEAN-US Business Council, Asia Society, Asian Institute of Management, Executive Council on Foreign Diplomats, Far East-American Council of Commerce and Industry, Foreign Policy Association, National Council for US-China Trade, Kennedy Center Corporate Fund.

BURGER, WARREN E(ARL) (1907–   ). Born, St. Paul, Minnesota; student, University of Minnesota, 1925–27; LL.B., magna cum laude, St. Paul College of Law (now William Mitchell College of Law); Doctor of Laws, 1931; honorary degrees, LL.D., William Mitchell College of Law, 1966, and New York Law School, 1976; admitted to Minnesota bar, 1931; faculty, William Mitchell College of Law, 1931–53; partner, Faricy, Burger, Moore & Costello (and predecessor firms), 1935–53; assistant attorney general in charge of Civil Division, US Department of Justice, 1953–56; judge of US Court of Appeals, District of Columbia, 1956–69; Chief Justice of the United States, 1969–   ; lecturer, American and European law schools; faculty, Appellate Judges Seminar, New York University Law School, 1958–   ; member and legal adviser to US delegation to International Labor Organization, Geneva, 1954; contributor to law journals and other publications. (See also *Current Biography*: November 1969).

CAREY, JAMES W. (1934–   ). Born, Providence, Rhode Island; B.A., University of Rhode Island, 1957; M.A., University of Illinois, 1959; Ph.D., University of Illinois, 1963; member, department of journalism, University of Illinois, 1963–69; professor, Journalism, and director of the Institute of Communications Research, 1969–76; dean, College of Communications, 1979–   ; George H.

Gallup Chair, University of Iowa, 1976–79; faculty, Pennsylvania State University, 1967–68; National Endowment for the Humanities Fellowship in Science, Technology, and Human Values, 1975; associate member, Center for Advanced Study, 1975; national accrediting council in journalism and communications, 1970–75; president, Association of Education in Journalism, 1977–78; author, more than sixty articles and reviews on the history of mass media, popular culture, and communication; member, editorial boards of several journals, lecturer at more than twenty-five American and European universities.

CARTER, JIMMY (JAMES EARL CARTER JR.) (1924–   ). Born, Plains, Georgia; student, Georgia Southwestern University, 1941–42; Georgia Institute of Technology, 1942–43; B.S., US Naval Academy, 1946; postgraduate instruction, nuclear physics, Union College, 1952; honorary degrees: Morris Brown College, Morehouse College, Notre Dame University and Georgia Institute of Technology; US Navy, 1947–53, advancing through grades to lieutenant commander; resigned 1953; farmer, warehouseman, 1953–77; served two terms in Georgia senate (Democrat), 1962–66 (voted most effective member); governor, 1971–74; chairman, Democratic National Campaign Committee, 1974; US President, 1977–81; past president, Georgia Planning Association; first chairman, West Central Georgia Planning and Development Commission; author; *Why Not the Best* (1975). (See also *Current Biography:* November 1977.)

ERVIN, SAMUEL JAMES JR. (1896–   ). Born, Morgantown, North Carolina; B.A. University of North Carolina 1917; LL.B. Harvard University, 1922; US Army, World War I, twice wounded and decorated for gallantry in action; admitted, North Carolina bar, 1919; representative, North Carolina General Assembly, 1923, 1925, 1931, 1937–43; associate justice, North Carolina Supreme Court, 1948–1954; representative, US Congress, 1946–47; US Senator, 1954–74; member, Senate Watergate committee; awards, nineteen honorary university degrees. (See also *Current Biography:* October 1973.)

HARRIS, PATRICIA ROBERTS (1924–   ). Born, Mattoon, Illinois; B.A., *summa cum laude,* Howard University, 1945; J.D., *cum laude,* George Washington University, 1960; post-graduate study, University of Chicago, 1945–47, and American University, 1949–50; program director, YWCA, Chicago, 1946–49; assistant director, American Council on Human Rights, 1949–53; executive director, Delta Sigma Theta, 1953–59; research associate, George Washington University School of Law, 1959–60; admitted, Supreme Court bar, 1960; trial attorney, Justice Department, 1960–61; associate dean of students, lecturer in law, Howard University, 1961–63; professor of law, 1963–65 and 1967–69; dean, School of Law, 1979; US Secretary, Department of Housing and Urban Development, 1977–80; Secretary, Health, Education, and Welfare, 1980; Secretary, Health and Human Services, 1980–81; US ambassador to Luxembourg, 1965–67; member, organizations: community relations, women's rights, civil rights, law reform, and the District of Columbia; awards, more than thirty-five honorary degrees, government of Luxembourg. (See also *Current Biography:* December 1965.)

JORDAN, VERNON E. JR. (1935–   ). Born, Atlanta, Georgia; B.A., DePauw University, 1957; first prize, Indiana Interstate Oratorical Contest, sophomore year; J.D., Howard University, 1960; honorary degrees from fifteen institutions; circuit vice president of American Law Students Association while at Howard University; helped to desegregate the University of Georgia; clerk in law office of civil rights attorney Donald Hollowell; field secretary, NAACP, Georgia branch, 1962; set up law partnership in Arkansas with another civil rights lawyer, Wiley A. Barnton, 1964; director, Voter Education Project for the Southern Regional Council, 1964–68; executive director, United Negro College Fund, 1970–72; director, National Urban League, January 1972–   ; member, Arkansas and Georgia bar associations; US Supreme Court bar; American Bar Association; Common Cause; Rockefeller Foundation; Twentieth Century Fund; other service organizatons; has held fellowships at Harvard University's Institute of Politics, the John F. Kennedy School of Government, and the Metropolitan Applied Research Center; serves on boards of several corporations. (See also *Current Biography:* February 1972.)

KENNEDY, EDWARD MOORE (1932–   ). Born, Boston, Massachusetts, B.A., Harvard University, 1956; student, International Law School, The Hague, The Netherlands, 1958; LL.B., University of Virginia, 1959; honorary degrees, thirteen institutions; admitted, Massachusetts bar, 1959; Assistant District Attorney, Suffolk County, Mass., 1961–62. US Senator, Massachusetts, 1962–   ; former Assistant Majority Leader, US Senate; president, Joseph P. Kennedy Jr. Foundation, 1961–   ; member board of trustees, universities, hospitals, libraries, the Boston Symphony, John F. Kennedy Center for the Performing Arts, and Robert F. Kennedy

Memorial Foundation; named one of ten outstanding young men
in US by Junior Chamber of Commerce, 1967; author, *Decisions
for a Decade, In Critical Condition;* Democratic candidate, US
President, 1980. (See also *Current Biography,* October 1978.)

KNAPP, DAVID CURTIS (1927–   ). Born, Syracuse, New York;
B.A., Syracuse University, 1947; M.A., 1948; Ph.D., University of
Chicago, 1953; assistant professor and professor of government,
University of New Hampshire, 1953–62; dean, College of Liberal
Arts, 1961–62; associate director, Study of American Colleges of
Agriculture, College Park, Maryland, 1963–65; director, Institute
of American College and University Administrators, American
Council on Education, 1965–68; dean, New York State College of
Human Ecology, 1968–74; provost, Cornell University, 1974–78;
president, University of Massachusetts, 1978–   ); Fulbright re-
search scholar, Finland, 1959–60; Bullard fellow, Graduate School
of Public Administration, Harvard University, 1962–63; US Army,
1950–52; member, American Political Science Association,
American Society for Public Administration, Phi Beta Kappa; author, with C. E. Kellogg, *The College of Agriculture: Science in the
Public Service,* 1964.

LAINGEN, LOWELL BRUCE (1922–   ). Born, Odin Township,
Minnesota; B.A. *cum laude* St. Olaf College, 1947; M.A. in international relations, University of Minnesota, 1949; international relations officer, US State Department, 1949–59; foreign service,
1950; in embassies, Hamburg, Germany, 1951–53, Teheran, Iran,
1953–54, Meshed, Iran, 1954–55, officer in charge of Greek affairs,
1956–60, Pakistan, 1960–64; assigned, national War College,
1967–68, American interests in Afghanistan, Bangladesh, India,
Nepal, Sri Lanka, the Maldives; ambassador to Malta, 1976;
Chargé d'affaires and the highest ranking official, US Embassy,
Teheran, 1979 during hostage crisis.

MAHONEY, DAVID JOSEPH JR. (1923–   ). Born, New York,
New York; LaSalle Military Academy, 1941; B.S., University of
Pennsylvania, 1945; student, Columbia University, 1946–47;
LL.D., Manhattan College; advertising vice president, Ruthrauff
& Ryan, Inc., 1949–51; founder and president, David J. Mahoney,
Inc., 1951–56; president and director, Good Humor Corporation,
1956–61; executive vice president and director, Colgate Palmolive
Company, 1961–66; president and chief executive officer, Canada
Dr. Corporation, 1966–68; president, 1968–69; president, director,
and chief executive officer, Norton Simon, Inc., 1969–   ; chair-

man, American Revolution Bicentennial Commission, 1976; director, American Health Foundation, Phoenix House, Madison Square Boys Club, the United Negro College Fund; trustee, New York University, University of Pennsylvania; awards, Torch of Liberty of Anti-Defamation League, 1970; Patriots award (Congressional Medal of Honor Society), 1972; Applause award (Sales Executive Club) 1973; US Marines Leatherneck award, 1975; Girl Scouts of America's Corporate Leadership award, 1976; named man of the year by *Advertising Age* and the Wharton School of Business, 1972.

MATHIAS, CHARLES McCURDY JR. (1922–   ). Born, Frederick, Maryland; US Navy, 1942–46; B.A., Haverford College, 1944; LL.B., University of Maryland, 1949; partner, Mathias, Mathias & Michel, Frederick, 1949–53; assistant attorney general of Maryland, 1953–54; city attorney, Frederick, 1954–59; member, House of Delegates, Maryland, 1958; partner, Niles, Barton, Markell and Gans, Baltimore, 1960–   ; member, US House of Representatives (Republican, Maryland), 1961–67; US Senate, 1968– (See also *Current Biography:* December 1972.)

QUAINTON, ANTHONY C. E. (1934–   ). Born, Seattle, Washington; B.A., Princeton University, 1955; B. of Letters, Oxford University, 1958; additional year at Oxford, research fellow, 1958–59; foreign service, Sydney, Australia, 1959; Karachi, 1963; Rawalpindi, 1964–66; New Delhi, 1966–69; senior political Officer, US Department of State, India, 1969–1972; Paris, 1972; deputy chief of mission, Kathmandu, 1973–76; ambassador, Central African Empire, 1976–78; director, Office for Combatting Terrorism, US Department of State, 1979–   ; English Speaking Union fellow, 1951–52; Marshall scholar, 1955–58; Rivkin award, 1972.

REAGAN, RONALD W(ILSON) (1911–   ). Born, Tampico, Illinois; B.A., Eureka College (Illinois) 1932; sports announcer, radio statin WHO, Des Moines, Iowa, 1932–37; motion picture and television actor, 1937–1966; program supervisor, General Electric Theater; president, Screen Actors Guild, 1947–52, 1959; captain, US Air Force, 1942–45; governor, California, 1967–74; unsuccessful candidate for Republican presidential nomination, 1976; Republican nominee and US President, 1980–   . (See also *Current Biography:* February 1967.)

SALDICH, ANNE RAWLEY (1933–   ). Born, Orange, New Jersey; B.A. *cum laude*, University of Detroit, 1958; M.A. *magna cum laude,* Wayne State University, 1962; Woodrow Wilson Fellowship, 1962; student, University of California at Berkeley, 1962–64; Ph.D. *mention bien,* University of Paris, 1971; teacher, College of Notre Dame (Belmont, California), history, politics, government, international relations, communications, 1962; College of San Mateo, 1965; San Jose University, 1972; University of Santa Clara, 1973; University of California, Berkeley, 1977; author, *Electronic Democracy: Television's Impact on the American Political Process,* articles in professional journals; assistant editor, *Journal of Economic Literature,* 1980–

SAWHILL, JOHN CRITTENDEN (1936–   ). Born, Cleveland, Ohio; B.A., Princeton University, 1958; Ph.D., New York University, 1963; director, Credit Research and Planning, Commercial Credit Company, 1964–66; associate, McKinsey & Company, Inc., 1966–68; senior vice president, Commercial Credit Company; member, Executive Committee, Control Data Corporation, 1968–72; associate director, Energy and Natural Resources, Office of Management and Budget, 1972–74; administrator, Federal Energy Administration, 1973–75; president, New York University, 1975–79; deputy secretary, Department of Energy, 1979–80; Chairman of the Board and Chief Executive Officer, US Synthetic Fuels Corporation, 1980–81; director, McKinsey & Company, Inc., 1981–

THIMMESCH, NICHOLAS "NICK" PADEN (1927–   ). Born, Dubuque, Iowa; B.A. University of Iowa, 1950; postgraduate work, 1955; reporter, Davenport (Iowa) *Times,* 1950–52; Des Moines (Iowa) *Register,* 1953–55: correspondent, *Time,* Inc., 1955–67; Washington bureau chief, *Newsday,* 1967–69; syndicated columnist, Los Angeles Times Syndicate, 1969–   ; contributing editor, *New York* magazine, 1977–78; co-author, with William Johnson, *The Bobby Kennedy Nobody Knows;* author, *The Condition of Republicanism,* articles in many national magazines; appearances on "Meet the Press," "Face the Nation," "Reporters' Roundup," the Voice of America: Public Broadcast Service network; member, president's commission, World Population Year, 1974; H. L. Mencken Society; National Advisory Council, St. John's University (Minnesota); fellow, Institute of Politics, John F. Kennedy School of Government, Harvard University, 1980–81.

CUMULATIVE SPEAKER INDEX

1980–1981

A cumulative author index to the volumes of REPRESEN-TATIVE AMERICAN SPEECHES for the years 1937–1938 through 1959–1960 appears in the 1959–1960 volume, for the years 1960–1961 through 1969–70 in the 1969–1970 volume, and for 1970–1971 through 1979–80 in the 1979–1980 volume.